"*Health Guardianship* i
wants to understand 
healthcare, but wants a solution. As an internationally respected surgeon and professor at a major medical center, Dr. Daneshgari achieved the pinnacle of academic medicine. From this unique position he gained a deep understanding the dysfunction of the American healthcare system. Through decades of study, he came to realize that American healthcare had morphed into a "sick care system" that no longer truly served the individual patient. Filled with powerful insight and analysis, *Health Guardianship* maps out a solution that can lower costs, improve outcomes, and place the patient back at the center of American medicine."

CL Gray, MD
President, Physicians for Reform

"From Professor of Surgery to Head of Department at one of the most famous hospitals in the country, Dr. Daneshgari is at the top. But transformation in the health care system has stubbornly refused to bend to those at the top, even when they are politicians trying to bring healthcare quality and access up while bringing the runaway costs down. *Health Guardianship* gives us a glimpse into delivering patient care that is genuinely affordable, accessible and of the highest quality."

Dr. Tony Dale
Founder and CEO of Sedera

"How do we transition our 'sick care system' to a real 'health system'? Firouz Daneshgari explains how our 'sick care' evolved and provides insights as to what he believes will expedite the transition to a real 'health system."

Thomas S. Campanella, JD, MA
Healthcare Executive in Residence

*Health Guardianship* is a must-read book for healthcare providers and consumers alike. Dr. Daneshgari correctly walks the reader through steps taken in the USA by both private industry and government that have led to the disastrously and unnecessarily expensive healthcare system we have today. He advances healthcare provider innovative ideas that streamline and realign financial incentives among providers and consumers in order to optimize quality of care while reducing waste of precious resources. More than that, Dr. Daneshgari has put these important innovations in practice leading to an emerging company that now puts these breakthrough ideas into daily practice. This book is thought-provoking and unparalleled in its scope.

John Fleming, MD
Former Deputy Assistant Secretary,
US Department of Health and Human Services

# HEALTH
GUARDIANSHIP

# HEALTH GUARDIANSHIP

## THE REMEDY TO THE SICK CARE SYSTEM

# FIROUZ DANESHGARI, M.D.
### WITH BERNARD EVENHUIS, MSIII

©2022 Firouz Daneshgari

All rights reserved. No part of this publication may be reproduced or transmitted in any form or by any means, electronic or mechanical, including photography, recording, or any information storage and retrieval system, without permission in writing from the author.

Requests for permission to make copies of any part of the work should be mailed to the following address: fd@bowtiemedical.com

Published and distributed by Merack Publishing.

Library of Congress Control Number: 2022917549

Health Guardianship: The Remedy to the Sick Care System

ISBN: Paperback 978-1-957048-64-2
ISBN: Hardcover 978-1-957048-66-6
ISBN: eBook 978-1-957048-65-9

To all those who taught me
a lesson in life.

# CONTENTS

Preface   1

Introduction   7

## PART I
## Formation of the 20th-Century Healthcare System   13

### CHAPTER 1
The 20th-Century American Healthcare System and Its Segments   15

### CHAPTER 2
Who Should Pay for the Cost of Healthcare?   25

### CHAPTER 3
Multiple-Payers and Providers of the U.S. Healthcare System   31

## PART II
## Report Card of the 20th-Century Healthcare System   37

### CHAPTER 1
The Most Expensive Healthcare System in the World   39

### CHAPTER 2
A Mispriced Healthcare with Poor Health Outcomes   43

### CHAPTER 3
A Hospital-Based Sick Care System Benefiting from Sickness of Population   55

### CHAPTER 4
Government Cost-Cutting Trials Don't Work   65

**PART III**
**Our Healthcare System Is Sick with Waste!**     71

    CHAPTER 1
    Abundance of Waste: The Primary Sign
    of Sickness in Healthcare     73

    CHAPTER 2
    The Hospital-Based Sick Care System Drives the Waste,
    and Insurance Companies Pay for It     81

    CHAPTER 3
    Waste Leads to Grave Medical Errors     85

    CHAPTER 4
    Waste is Cloaked from the Consumer     91

**PART IV**
**The Root Cause of Perpetual Waste:**     **95**

    CHAPTER 1
    The Misalignment between Financial
    Incentives of Providers     97

    CHAPTER 2
    The Misalignment between the Payers
    and the Providers     105

    CHAPTER 3
    The Misalignment between Intermediaries     109

**PART V**
**Changes of Life in the 21st Century**
**that Demand Change in Healthcare Delivery**     **113**

    CHAPTER 1
    Democratization and Demonetization
    of Health Information     115

    CHAPTER 2
    Telemedicine and Virtual Delivery of Care     119

CHAPTER 3
Biomedical Technology                                     123

CHAPTER 4
Artificial Intelligence                                   129

# PART VI
**SARS-CoV-2 Pandemic Lessons for Our Healthcare**        **133**

CHAPTER 1                                                 135

# PART VII
**How to Fix the System and Not Bandage It?**             **147**

CHAPTER 1
Reduce the Waste by Fixing the Misalignments              149

CHAPTER 2
Reward Guardianship of Health,
Not Delivery of Sick Care Services                        153

CHAPTER 3
Free to Choose! Consumers MUST Be
in Control of Their Money!                                155

CHAPTER 4
Disrupt the System toward Healthcare
and Away from Sick Care!                                  161

# PART VIII
**Health Guardianship: The New and Missing
Piece for a Post-Pandemic Healthcare System**             **165**

CHAPTER 1
Fill the Existing Gap between Public Health
and the Hospital-Based Sick Care System                   167

CHAPTER 2
Chronic Conditions MUST GO!
The Moonshot Is Possible                                  171

**CHAPTER 3**
Health Risk Management Instead of
Disease Management — 177

**CHAPTER 4**
A Bow-Tie Risk Management Segment for Healthcare — 181

**CHAPTER 5**
How Would the New Segment of
Health Guardianship Work? — 185

**CHAPTER 6**
Health Guardians Would Integrate
Health Risk Management — 191

**CHAPTER 7**
BowTie Health Guardianship Moonshot: — 199

Epilogue — 203

Appendices — 207

Appendix — 215

Bibliography — 217

Acknowledgments — 237

About the Author — 239

# PREFACE

As a rising-star academician and a newly appointed chairman of a prestigious surgical subspecialty in a major academic hospital—and after an energetic presentation to the hospital's board—I was appointed to the strategic committee of the board of directors of a healthcare system comprising 11 hospitals, 100 outpatient facilities, over 200 clinics, nearly 30,000 employees, and an annual revenue of nearly $3 billion. Blessed with this position of influence, I was excited to funnel my efforts toward making meaningful change in American healthcare at large.

However, I quickly realized that my understanding of the operations and dynamics within the American healthcare system differed greatly from that of the other board members. My fellow board members came largely from business and financial management backgrounds. And, while I focused on healthcare goals through improving patient care and physician training, the rest of the board prioritized the financial metrics of initiatives brought to our table. To understand why our priorities differed, I began to research the development of hospital boards and their governance structures. Taking a historical approach, I discovered how the American hospital structure evolved from charity houses in the late 19th century to the current oligopolistic, multibillion-dollar financial institutions present today.

I also discovered that the American healthcare system had become the most expensive system in the world, spending 300%–500% more than similar nations, but trailing those nations in patient outcomes. As a renowned professor and surgeon, I traveled the world and operated in many countries, and I witnessed the differences between our healthcare and that of other nations. I noticed that, despite its disproportionate price tag, the American healthcare system lacked a competitive edge in positive health outcomes. As a result, our country consistently ranked between 30th and 40th in the World Health Organization's ratings for patient longevity, access to care, and prevalence of chronic conditions. I began to wonder about the causes of our healthcare system's deficiencies. Why were we spending so much more, but getting so little in return?

Despite my years of experience in basic science and clinical research, I realized that I lacked the tools to even begin investigating these topics. I needed to acquire the fundamentals of business research and surround myself with an environment conducive to this line of questioning. So, I enrolled into the executive MBA program at the university where I was a clinical department chair. There, I shared ideas with some of the most brilliant and informed innovators in business. And, combining my newfound business knowledge with a lifelong clinical background, I began to see the problem more clearly.

In the world of business, everyone knew that our healthcare system was "sick." They had done the research, and significant volumes of publications on "signs and symptoms" of this sickness were referenced daily in conversations. The prime example of this sickness is that "medical errors" have risen to the third most common cause of death in the United States, trailing only behind heart disease and cancer.

But with this new observation, my focus shifted away from describing these signs and symptoms toward a different line of questioning. How could our healthcare system be fixed? How could we make it more affordable for our nation, while improving patient outcomes such as better access to care, and a lower incidence of chronic conditions? Could we model a solution after existing approaches in other nations, while still meeting the demands of American society with its diverse geographical and cultural differences?

Channeling my clinical research training, I knew the next step was to characterize the "pathophysiology" of this sickness. In other words, what processes and factors became dysfunctional to create the symptoms that we experience? There were a few key questions.

1) How did 5,000 hospitals become the primary mode of healthcare delivery in the American healthcare system, while benefiting from the business of sick care and sickness of the population?

2) How and why have employers and the government become the two largest payers for healthcare? Why don't Americans pay directly for their healthcare when direct, buyer-to-seller payment methods have led to optimized prices for cars, houses, food, and other needs in the free markets of other industries?

3) How and why has the individual consumer (the American citizen) lost control over her own healthcare, and become the victim of its outrageous prices and dysfunctional services?

To answer these questions, I knew I needed to create an environment outside of the sick care system where I could perform this line of inquiry unperturbed. I needed a major change in my career. So, I founded a healthcare startup company dedicated to finding remedies to the ills of the American healthcare system, and I left my position as hospital department chair.

Then the COVID-19 pandemic struck, wreaking havoc on our communities and our already fragile healthcare system. It was not until I observed the beginning of this pandemic, and our country's failed attempts at defending citizens' health against the virus, that I discovered this book's central finding.

In American healthcare, there is a wide gap between the services provided by the hospital-based sick care system and that of public health. The sick care system administers care when we are already sick, and the departments of public health issue orders and mandates regarding how to behave during a health crisis. Between these two; however, we simply do not have a system that focuses on and benefits from protecting and maintaining our health. To fill this gap, and to heal our sick care system, we must establish a new institution that truly protects, invests in, and benefits from our health and longevity. This institution would:

I. Bridge the gap between services of public health and hospital-based sick care by providing individualized services to keep us healthy. This is the key to lowering the staggering cost of healthcare: to maintain and improve our health so that the services of the sick care system are not needed in the first place. The financial resources freed from this measure alone could then be reinvested into more productive pursuits, creating a nation that is both healthier and wealthier.

II. Reduce or eliminate the prevalence of chronic conditions, such as obesity or diabetes. COVID-19 showed us that the high prevalence of these conditions is not merely the subject of academic debate, but actual causes of death in nearly half a million Americans killed by COVID-19.

III. Restore the consumer of American healthcare to the position of an engaged and empowered customer. If the American citizen controls market demand through their own purchase preferences, they may drive competition, efficiency, and quality across the entire healthcare industry as they have done in every other industry.

IV. Create and enforce efficiency in the hospital-based sick care system by comparing prices and patient outcomes (instead of artwork on hospital walls) when the services of sick care are needed.

I wrote this book to inform any person interested in American healthcare about the findings that I'm privileged to have made. I have enjoyed this journey of question and discovery for the past several years, and I am pleased to have found a solution to bridging this damaging gap. As you read through these pages, I hope you can experience and enjoy the same journey just as much. As a surgeon-scientist, I read new discoveries every day about extending the longevity of the human being past lengths we previously thought impossible. And it has become apparent that our bodies have the biological capacity to live a full life, beyond 100 years old, if only we have the proper institutions to help us to maintain and improve our health. Let's shoot for this goal by establishing this new segment of American healthcare: the Health Guardianship.

Firouz Daneshgari, MD, MBA, FPMRS, FACS
Summer of 2022

# INTRODUCTION

An overwhelming majority of Americans (>92%) agree that our healthcare system is "sick" and is in need of significant change. Almost everyone has a personal story of experiencing a few symptoms of that sickness. There have also been many books written exploring the specific dysfunctions in the healthcare system and how they could be fixed. Here are common themes:

1. The current American healthcare system is the most expensive and wasteful system we have ever had. The cost of healthcare is no longer affordable by our government, employers, or citizens.

2. Some of the sharpest minds in the world work in our healthcare system, and this has led to incredible technological advancements in medicine. However, while technological advances in other industries such as transportation, communication, food, etc., have made those services more accessible and affordable,

advances in this industry have made healthcare more expensive and unaffordable.

3. The healthcare system in the United States has become the largest industry in the country. This industry is built upon a long-standing and somehow sacred relationship between a patient and a doctor, the two pillars of healthcare. But over the past 70–80 years, a set of intermediaries have inserted themselves between these two pillars and have made healthcare unaffordable for the patient and intolerable for the doctor. Intermediaries include insurance companies, the hospitals, the government, the employers, and a whole host of brokers and administrators who are eager to make healthcare better for those two pillars, yet often make it worse. Currently, there are at least 10 intermediaries for every doctor and patient in the healthcare system!

4. Who is to blame? Is it the insurance companies, the government, the drug companies, the hospitals, or the American citizens who are reluctant to adopt healthy habits or prudent healthcare spending practices? Within this topic, there is a significant political divide that sometimes leads to shouting matches from presidential debates to media scenes.

I'm not a politician or a scholar on the history of political systems. However, I vividly remember the fall of the Soviet Union and its surrounding political systems. Back then, we saw the truth in plain view: when a system is dysfunctional, it will fall to its own complications.

After having spent my entire adult life working in hospitals, it was such an irony to discover that although most hospitals in the U.S. are not-for-profit, every major healthcare system routinely reports double-digit net profits. During the writing of this book, the Cleveland Clinic announced a $1.3 billion net income during the first six months of 2021, and Mass General reported a $1.1 billion net income during the first quarter of 2022. These are only two examples of a long list of very profitable institutions.

During the past presidential election cycles, we have targeted insurance companies, Big Pharma, medical device manufacturers, and other components of healthcare as single causes of our system's dysfunction. Playing this blame game has widened the political divide and blinded us to the true problems of our healthcare system. A dysfunctional system will ultimately fall to its own complications, whether it be a communist regime, an organization (remember Enron Corporation?), or a healthcare system. And to solve this dysfunction, one must address systemic problems instead of blaming individual components within that system. Fixing one piece does not address the overall dysfunction: when a system is fundamentally misaligned in its design, the components of that system contribute to the problem perpetually.

Today, we know that the former Soviet Union had a major systemic flaw: that no Big Brother supervision or control can replace the motivation and creativity of an individual who aims to create prosperity for himself and his community. Similarly, no top-down approach to healthcare by the government (single-payer), insurance, or hospitals (managed care) can serve as a substitute for the self-governing ability of a person who is motivated to live a healthy and productive life, and to look after her own financial well-being.

Equipped with these simple beliefs, I toured around the world to visit various healthcare systems in pursuit of a solution for the maladies of our healthcare. During this journey, I encountered Dr. Gustove, the coordinator of healthcare in São Paulo, Brazil. He shared some powerful advice with me, "The solution for your healthcare system is in innovation toward the next model that must be born from your existing system. No existing model in the world would solve the systemic ailments of your healthcare system."

To understand the root causes of dysfunction in American healthcare, I will begin by describing how the components of our current healthcare system came together at the beginning of the 20th century. Afterwards, I will describe the results of that healthcare system: its cost, outcomes, and problems. Next, we will review advances brought to our lives in the 21st century and how they may contribute to solutions for the future. We will briefly discuss the milestones traversed in democratizing medical and health information through technology and the internet, and the increased utilization of virtual care delivery models. We will also reflect on the COVID-19 pandemic, and review lessons this health crisis has taught us as a nation.

Next, I will describe the rationale for the establishment of a new segment of our healthcare system: Health Guardianship. This segment that will focus solely on our health, mitigation of health risks, and elimination of chronic conditions. This segment will be more a "health care" complimenting the current sick care and public health systems. I will describe how Health Guardianship can be built from the existing primary care infrastructure with integration of virtual health, wellness services, and price transparency tools. I will also demonstrate how these provisions would make Health Guardianship as accessible, affordable, and consumer centric as retail shopping, communication, traveling, and many of our other needs.

This book is based on more than 30 years of research by a number of top institutions and thought-leaders, who have published their findings in peer-reviewed journals as well as public outlets. I have meticulously studied these resources, connected the dots, and explored the systemic problems at the root of dysfunction in U.S. healthcare.

I struggled to find a conclusive answer when I noted the fact that during the early years of the 21st century "medical errors" have become the third leading cause of death in the U.S. It was the COVID-19 pandemic that opened my eyes to the answer: we have built a system specialized for sick care, and yet ironically we expect the results of "healthcare" from it. The fundamental problem in healthcare is not attributable to any single component, but rather misalignments among the components of the current system that promote sick care and are benefiting from it. We must fix these misalignments, so the components that currently contribute to the problem can instead be a part of the solution toward healthcare.

It is only after these systematic misalignments are corrected that the great technological advances in American medicine, training of some of the best doctors in the world, new drug discoveries, robotic surgery, identification of genetic risk factors, and the many other biomedical innovations our country has developed, can lead to 'good health', the ultimate desired output of healthcare.. But as long as the system remains misaligned, these sources of excitement and discovery, and all the human effort that fuels them, will not lead to better healthcare or even healthier lives.

The good news is that correction of these misalignments is within reach. Several startup companies have already begun the initial buds of disruptive innovation in that direction, and a few simple regulatory changes will accelerate the process.

Through this paradigm shift, we may channel unparalleled American ingenuity, innovation, and effort toward a reformed healthcare system that provides 'good health' for every American and may serve as a role model for healthcare systems throughout the globe.

# PART I
# FORMATION OF THE 20TH-CENTURY HEALTHCARE SYSTEM

CHAPTER 1

# THE 20TH-CENTURY AMERICAN HEALTHCARE SYSTEM AND ITS SEGMENTS

The roots of medicine can be traced back to 2600 BC, when the Egyptian Imhotep described the diagnosis and treatment of 200 different diseases;[1] to Herophilus, the father of anatomy, who performed the first-ever dissection on the human body;[2] and to the birth of Hippocrates, the Greek father of medicine who began the study of medical science and prescribed a form of aspirin to women in childbirth.[3] The use of medications to treat illness can be traced back to ancient Mesopotamia, as artifacts from the Sumer civilization depict opium poppy[4] and refer to it as the "joy plant" for its euphoric effects and ability to soothe people.[5]

Throughout the development of medicine, there has been an important overlap between religion and medicine. The confluence of these two domains was seen as early as ancient Egypt, where the "medicine man" and "religious man" shared the same position.[6] This position came with privilege: Egyptian healers had the pride of being buried with pharaohs to ensure that they could serve their kings in the afterlife. The roles of "doctor" and "religious leader" were unified because it was the shared understanding of early civilizations that illness was a part of the gods' response to human behavior. People would pray for the wellbeing of the sick in a practice that still remains today. Consequently, religious communities have always expressed a commitment to care for the poor and sick. The connection between these two domains has culminated in the major role religious institutions have played in the transformation of healthcare throughout history and in the delivery of healthcare today.

American healthcare has also participated in connecting religion and medicine. We may see this most evidently in the cultural attitudes of our WWI and WWII generations, who have elevated American doctors above normal human ethics, with the power over health and illness, joy and pain, life and death—nearly as "gods" in themselves. Though this cultural attitude has fostered national trust in physicians, it has also created a vacuum, free from the checks and balances that stabilize any capitalistic system. Consequently, this view of doctors has fostered an ignorance of systemic misalignments that have been introduced into our healthcare system over the past few decades. We will review the development of these misalignments later in this book.

## A Place for Recovery: From Homes to the Hospitals

The major medical demands in earlier societies consisted of tending to the needs of the sick and those injured in wars and accidents. This issue led to the establishment of designated places where the injured could be healed. In early 19th-century France, Napoleon established centers for his soldiers to recover after they were injured in his many wars.[7]

In 1752, the U.S. opened its first hospitals, dedicated to treating medical conditions.[8] When the Industrial Revolution struck from about 1760 to 1840, it encouraged advancements in the sophistication and complexity of medicine. During the civil war (1861–1865), further progress was made in American medicine. As a consequence, it started to make less sense for families and community members to care for the sick at home.[6] The transfer of caretaking responsibilities from family members at home to hospitals became the norm toward the end of the 19th century. Diagnostic technologies such as X-rays, laboratory tests, and bacterial cultures were offered alongside therapeutic interventions such as surgery, wound care, antibiotic therapies, and blood transfusion. The intersection of these advancements made hospitals the ideal location for taking care of the sick.

## Leading Causes of Death Drive the Formation of Public Health and a Hospital-Based Delivery System

As hospitals and medical centers became recognized as sites for caring for the ill, the attention of scientific and medical communities turned toward identifying leading causes of hospitalizations and death. During the late 19th century, the leading cause of death was infectious disease.[9] This recognition encouraged academic societies to focus on causes of common infectious diseases including tuberculosis, cholera, diphtheria, smallpox, whooping cough, and others. With advancements in microbiology and identification of mechanisms that spread infectious diseases, it became apparent that many of the diseases were preventable. Consequently, hospitals and medical centers began to transform part of their work toward preventative measures that required community, population-level, and national strategies.

The adoption of these strategies required a separation between hospitals and population-level initiatives, and some physicians and scientists began to specialize in infectious disease epidemiology and public health. At the same time, the medical community increasingly recognized that the contamination of water, food, and other resources could lead to the spread of infectious disease and result in a pandemic. The emergence of public health brought to the forefront a necessity to control these sources of disease. Some medical centers in larger cities like New York, Boston, and Baltimore transformed into departments of public health, taking on the primary responsibility of educating the government and public on how to prevent the spread of infectious diseases.

## A. Public Health: To Protect the Public from Communicable Diseases

The origin of the public health system can be traced to the 1798 establishment of a system of Marine hospitals. In 1870, these were consolidated into the Marine Hospital Service,[14] and shortly afterwards the position of Surgeon General[15] and the Public Health Service Commissioned Corps (PHSCC)[12] were established. From that point on, public health has developed into three levels: federal, state, and local. At the federal level, the United States Public Health Service (USPHS) is organized as a division of the Department of Health and Human Services[10] that is overseen by the Assistant Secretary for Health (ASH),[11] whereas the Public Health Service Commissioned Corps (PHSCC)[12] is the federal uniformed service of the USPHS, functioning as one of the eight uniformed services of the United States.[13,16]

The PHSCC includes officers drawn from many professions, including environmental and occupational health, medicine, nursing, dentistry, pharmacy, psychology, social work, hospital administration, health record administration, nutrition, engineering, science, veterinary medicine, health information technology, and other health-related occupations.[18] Officers of the Corps wear uniforms similar to those of the United States Navy, with special PHSCC insignia,[21] and the Corps use the same commissioned officer ranks[22] as the U.S. Navy and Coast Guard. Service in the PHSCC is considered military service for retirement purposes, as it serves the good of the public.

The local levels of public health preceded the formation of state health departments. Baltimore, Maryland established the first city health department in 1793.[25] Afterward, state health agencies developed in Massachusetts and spread across the country during the latter half of the 19th century.[26] Demand for more health departments was fueled by a cultural ambivalence about federal government control, as well as a desire for local government intervention in sanitation and control of communicable diseases. Consequently, several more health departments were formed in the first half of the 20th century. By 2000, there were state health agencies in every state, and approximately 2,832 local health departments nationwide. State health departments, and many local health departments, developed and evolved independently. As a result, health departments vary considerably from state to state and community to community in their organizational structure, responsibilities, funding mechanisms, performance of core services and competencies, and implications for agency accreditation and workforce certification.

The National Association of County and City Health Officials (NACCHO)[28] represents 2,800 local public health departments in the United States. The NACCHO, which in collaboration with the Centers for Disease Control and Prevention (CDC),   •    is concerned with health, and has responsibility over the health of specific jurisdictions within each state.

As we will learn later from the lessons of the COVID-19 pandemic, much improvement in the operations and funding of the century-old structure of public health may be needed to thoroughly allow it to serve its mission of protecting the health of the U.S. population from common or communicable diseases.

## B. *The Hospital: A Place to Diagnose and Treat Diseases*

The late 19th and early 20th centuries ushered forth a number of discoveries that transformed the scope and capabilities of clinical medicine forever. Even before the development of anesthesia, which made advanced surgeries feasible, came the use of blood transfusions.[29] This advancement provided an incredibly vital element in surgery and trauma care by replacing the blood loss that inevitably accompanies advanced procedures. This effectively sustained the life of the patient.

In 1818 a British obstetrician performed the first successful blood transfusion using human blood to save a woman experiencing a postpartum hemorrhage.[29] About a hundred years later, scientists and physicians began studying blood types and cross-matching those blood types to find better-suited blood donors. In 1907 the first blood transfusion using cross-matching was successfully performed. Later, during WWII, the United States established the first blood collection program in order to aid the military. The Red Cross collected "more than 13 million pints" to aid survival for those injured in battle.[29] Today, medical practitioners use blood transfusion routinely to replace blood in a clinical setting.

As the 19th century concluded, Dr. Roentgen accidentally discovered the X-ray, paving the way for imaging in medical diagnostics.[30] In 1895, the physicist was testing whether or not a cathode ray could pass through glass. As he tested his hypothesis, he found a mysterious, green light illuminating on the other side of the glass. With further experimentation, he realized these rays could also pass through human tissue, leaving an image of bones underneath. The public met these findings with acclaim, and places as mundane as shoe stores soon allowed customers to take an x-ray of their feet to see the bones within. Later discoveries would prove how detrimental this access was, and thousands of people subsequently suffered the harmful side effects of radiation.

The first official surgical procedure that used anesthesiology was in 1846[31] when William T.G. Morton, a Boston dentist, used sulfuric ether to soothe a man when he needed a tumor removed from his neck. This was no minor feat: Anesthesia opened the possibility to perform surgery to fix anatomical or functional abnormalities, remove tumors, stop bleeding, remove obstruction, and many other surgical interventions. As a result, the field of surgery started to expand in the first half of the 20th century, diversifying into specialities such as cardiothoracic, vascular, urology, orthopedic, and neurosurgery. This expansion was further compounded by the development of subspecialities within each specialty, including surgical oncology and endocrine surgery within the general surgery specialty; pediatric surgery subspecialties within most surgical specialities; and even some subspecialties shared between surgical specialities, such as transplant surgery and female pelvic reconstructive surgery.

Recognized as established centers for treating complex diseases, hospitals rapidly absorbed these advances in medical imaging, surgery, chemotherapy, and other novel therapies. With this came an ever-increasing cost of hospitalization. Hospitals soon stratified into tiers, with lower tiers comprising small community hospitals lacking advanced medical technology and higher tiers featuring large academic medical centers capable of specialized, complex care. As we will review later, the number of hospitals grew to nearly 10,000 after World War II. This stratification of hospitals created a road map for their consolidation in the late 20th century toward establishment of health systems that included a combination of larger referral and smaller community hospitals.

CHAPTER 2

# WHO SHOULD PAY FOR THE COST OF HEALTHCARE?

For the public health segment, this question had an easy answer: governments at federal, state, and local levels pay for the cost of public health departments through general taxes, as it pertains to "health of the public."

The funding system today establishes budgets for public health departments based on a percentage of national health spending, national gross domestic product (GDP), total dollars spent, or dollars spent per capita.[32] Annual federal public health expenditures average 0.08% of GDP, 1.5% of federal health spending, and 0.5% of total health-related expenditures within both public and private sectors.

How is this budget made? At the federal level, Congress passes an appropriations bill or a continuing resolution that is signed into law by the President. The CDC then distributes the apportioned money to each state. Some city health departments also receive funds directly from the CDC, though there is a strict limit to this group. Finally, state health departments pass funds received from federal investments and state general funds to local departments of public health.

For the hospital-based segment; however, the answer was not so easy. Expensive technological advancements accumulated in hospitals, and this made payment for hospital services more expensive and unaffordable for most American families. In the early 1900s, religious organizations and other groups established charity hospitals with a mission of helping the poor. These were funded primarily through public subscriptions, bequests, and philanthropic donations. Similarly, community and teaching hospitals were established and paid for through the efforts of community leaders, which were relying on philanthropic contributions and patient fees procured through medical services.[7] Other hospitals were often sponsored by state or local governments and public initiatives with the specific goal of taking care of orphans, the elderly, and those with disabilities.

Throughout the 19th and 20th centuries, the United States lacked a unified approach to funding hospitals due to varying geographical, political, and state needs. Over time, the nation demanded a mechanism to fund community hospitals at the federal level. The peak of this effort resulted in the Hill-Burton

Act[33] that was signed into law by President Harry S. Truman on August 13, 1946. This act provided federal funding to establish one hospital bed for every 1,000 Americans. By 1975, the Hill-Burton Act was responsible for the construction of nearly one-third of U.S. hospitals. By the turn of the century, about 6,800 facilities in 4,000 communities had in some part been financed by this law, including not only hospitals and clinics, but also rehabilitation centers and long-term care facilities.

## Employers Pay for Most of the Working Americans: A Wartime Serendipity That Stuck

The role of hospitals in medical care grew steadily, and the wave of technological advancement in hospitals accompanied the growth of the costs. To keep up with the expense of new medical technology, and medical personnel to operate it, hospitals resorted to larger fees for medical services. Thus, the cost of hospitals became less affordable for the average citizen. This struggle was further intensified when the Great Depression struck in 1929.

The fee-for-service model that funded part of the hospital's expenses began to change in 1929 with a program implemented by Baylor Hospital in Dallas, Texas. A group of teachers in Dallas struck a deal with Baylor Hospital to cover any expenses they may incur from getting sick. They got a simple rate ($6 per year) and their hospital expenses would be covered. This plan became Blue Cross. In the 1930s, the lumber and mining industries combined efforts to provide basic physician services to their employees. This became Blue Shield. Thus, a hospital insurance plan and a medical insurance plan for basic coverage were created.[34]

Along with this development, WWII fundamentally altered a lot of the ways Americans engaged with healthcare. During the war, a demand for almost everything, particularly labor, climbed. In response, Congress passed the Stabilization Act of 1942. The Stabilization Act allowed President Franklin D. Roosevelt (FDR) to freeze the wages and salaries of all the nation's workers.[35] As a result, employers had little to offer their employees in terms of benefits and incentives. However, health insurance and pensions were two key exemptions in the Stabilization Act: FDR determined that these two areas could reasonably and modestly increase even while wages were frozen.

During this same year, the Revenue Act of 1942 was also passed. This fundamentally changed the tax structure in the United States by increasing individual income and corporate tax rates.[36] As with the Stabilization Act, the Revenue Act had an exception for health insurance. Corporations were therefore faced with a question with far-reaching consequences: do they pay for their employee's healthcare or pay the same amount of money in taxes? The Stabilization Act created a landscape with few ways to incentivize employee retention, and so the answer was clear. Immediately, the prevalence of employer-sponsored health insurance skyrocketed.

Following WWII, the IRS recognized employer-sponsored health insurance as a legitimate expense for businesses, without introducing tax consequences for employees.[37] In one stroke, this solidified the role of employers as purchasers of health insurance and thereby "payers" for the healthcare system. Employers soon became the largest private purchasers of health insurance in the U.S., and they have continued to hold this position even today. Employers are currently estimated to purchase 55%–68% of all health insurance in the nation, covering over 200 million workers and their dependents, or over half the country's population.[38]

## The Government Pays for Older, Disabled, Low-Income Adults and for Children

The debate to establish and expand a single-payer healthcare system in the U.S. has lasted for almost a century. Following the end of WWII in 1945, President Harry Truman followed FDR's efforts to provide single-payer healthcare to the nation, mimicking the dominant model in Europe.[39] The majority of European nations had pursued a government-sponsored model that created single-payer systems (in Germany, France, and Italy) and a single-payer/single-provider system (in England). These government-sponsored systems followed the "Bismarck model," which had the namesake of Otto von Bismarck, the esteemed Chancellor of Germany in the late 19th century.[43]

The Truman proposal was included as a part of the Social Security expansion, but the general public feared an increase in taxes and a resulting increase in control by the federal government. These fears were particularly publicized by the American Medical Association (AMA) and the American

Hospital Association (AHA), who lobbied to defeat President Truman's proposal for single-payer healthcare.[39] After Truman's efforts for national health insurance failed, advocates began to focus on the most needy part of the population: the elderly. In 1960, Congress passed the Kerr-Mills Act, which set up a federal-state matching program for poor Americans aged 65 and older. This created the plan for what became Medicaid, which had to be adopted by states, the last of which was Arizona in 1982.

Although President Kennedy advocated for Medicare during his short term in office, it was not a reality until July of 1965, when President Lyndon B. Johnson signed the Social Security Amendments Act. This established Medicare as a health insurance program for the elderly and Medicaid as a health insurance program for the impoverished and those with major disabilities such as renal failure and blindness.[40] The retired President Truman became the recipient of the very first Medicare card!

With the defeat of the single-payer healthcare proposal and the ratification of Medicare and Medicaid, the two largest payers of American health insurance were born: employers and the government. Today, over 200 million working-age Americans receive employer sponsored healthcare,[41] and nearly 100 million receive insurance through Medicare and Medicaid programs administered by Centers for Medicare & Medicaid Services.[42]

CHAPTER 3

# MULTIPLE-PAYERS AND PROVIDERS OF THE U.S. HEALTHCARE SYSTEM

The events of the 20th century determined the fate of American healthcare as a multiple-payer and multiple-provider system.

## Payer System: Convoluted and Masked Payments

The Multiple-Payer Segment of the U.S. system includes the following sources:

1. The federal government[44] sponsors Medicare for the elderly, Medicaid for those who qualify as low-income, the Children's Health Insurance Program (CHIP), the Veteran Administration[45] for

retired military, and the Department of Defense for Active Military. Through these programs, the U.S. federal government sponsors nearly 138 million Americans, or 42.8% of the population.[46]

2. State governments fund Medicaid and CHIP programs through a shared sponsorship with the federal government.

3. Employers provide coverage for 221 million Americans, or 68.5% of the population, through group and non-group insurance (individual and self-employed).

The following table shows the sources of payer coverage for the U.S. population in 2020, based on the Congressional Research Service:[46]

| Source of Coverage | Payer Source | Enrollment (millions/percentage of US population) |
|---|---|---|
| Private Health Insurance | Group-Employer Sponsored | 179 (55.4%) |
| Private Health Insurance | Non-Group | 42 (13.1%) |
| Medicare | Federal Government | 58 (18.1%) |
| Medicaid/CHIP | Federal and States | 64 (19.8%) |
| Military: TRICARE | DoD | 9 (2.7%) |
| Military: VA Care | DoD | 7 (2.2%) |
| Uninsured | N/A | 30 (9.2%) |
| TOTAL Insured | | 293 (90.8%) |

## Payment Methodology

The payment methodology adopted by this system is one of the most convoluted payment methods in the world. In general, there are two payment systems:

a. Medicare Level Payment: This method (also known as Medicare Fee Schedule) is executed through the Centers for Medicare & Medicaid Services (CMS). It has become increasingly complex (very similar to tax codes) with each successive administration, as well as yearly Medicare fee schedule changes. The fee schedule is calculated through a complex set of coding specifications, including International Codes of Diagnoses (ICD) for diagnoses of conditions, Current Procedural Terminology (CPT) for treatment procedures, and Related Value Units (RVUs) for calculating payments to physicians.

b. Commercial Level Payment: Payments by the private insurance companies are the wild west! Every insurance company establishes its own payment schedules with each provider (large or small) through a direct and mostly secret contract. The prices that are agreed upon between the providers (who are mostly hospitals) and insurance companies are hidden from everyone, including the consumer who ultimately foots the bill. As we will see later, in contrast to any free market discipline, the prices of medical services are never disclosed, discussed, or negotiated between the provider of those services and the consumer who pays. Further, the level of payment differs between government and commercial payers, even though they use the same RVUs, ICD, or CPT codes for calculating payments. An executive order issued by President Trump in 2020 (called "America First Healthcare Plan") has directed CMS to deliver regulations to create transparency of prices for the hospitals and payments by insurance companies. It is too early to judge the impact of these regulations.

## Payment Buckets

In addition to multiple-payers (government vs. employers) and multiple payment methodologies (Medicare vs. Commercial), there are also multiple buckets into which the cost of healthcare services is divided. These buckets include premiums paid by the sponsor (government or employer) versus the consumer, deductibles, copays, and coinsurance. The net effect of these numerous divisions, and this complex system at large, is a lack of transparency on the TOTAL cost of care for the consumer. Regardless of what direct costs are covered by patients versus their sponsors (government or employer), the individual consumer ultimately pays for the total cost of healthcare services through her wages, taxes, or directly from her pocket.[47]

## Provider System: A Hospital-Controlled Delivery System

The multiple-provider system is dominated by the presence of nearly 5,000 hospitals creating a hospital-based healthcare delivery system in the United States. Review of data released by the CMS and other agencies on healthcare spending shows at least one-third, about 38%, of the payments goes directly to the hospitals. However, the other categories of spending (i.e, payments to doctors (26%), prescription medications (14%), and other related services) are also indirectly controlled or influenced by the hospitals as the employers of doctors and other providers whose clinical decisions determine spending on most other categories. Therefore, hospitals and their employees influence more than 78% of the spending in U.S. healthcare based on data shown in the table below for 2020.

| Type of Provider | Percentage of Total Spending |
| --- | --- |
| Direct Payments to Hospitals | 38.3% |
| Doctors and Other Professional Services | 26.5% |
| Prescription Drugs and Other Medical Nondurables | 13.8% |
| Nursing Homes | 6.0% |
| Dental Services | 4.4% |
| Home Healthcare | 3.3% |
| Medical Durables | 1.8% |
| Health Residential and Personal Care | 5.9% |

As a part of its annual reporting, the CMS' Office of the Actuary estimated that total cost of healthcare spending reached $3.81 trillion in 2019 and would increase to $4.01 trillion in 2020. CMS projected that by 2028, healthcare spending would reach $6.19 trillion, and would account for 19.7% of GDP, up from 17.7% in 2018.[48]

In summary, developments in the 20th century created two main segments of healthcare in the U.S.: 1) public health, which aimed to prevent communicable diseases mostly through government funding; and 2) a multiple-payer, multiple-provider healthcare system funded by employers and taxes, and delivered through a hospital-based healthcare delivery system.

# PART II
## REPORT CARD OF THE 20TH-CENTURY HEALTHCARE SYSTEM

CHAPTER 1

# THE MOST EXPENSIVE HEALTHCARE SYSTEM IN THE WORLD

In the previous section, we discussed the structure and development of the American healthcare system. We will now turn to the results of this system. Over the past century, and especially over the past few decades, the healthcare expenditure in the U.S. has rapidly increased, consuming nearly 20% of the nation's entire production capacity, or GDP.

Between 1980 and 2018, the United States' spending on healthcare skyrocketed by 290% per person.[54] According to the CMS, this trend is not slowing down: by 2028, national health spending will reach $6.2 trillion.[48] To put this unfathomably large figure into perspective, the dollar amount we spend on healthcare within a year would reach nearly a third of the nation's GDP. The Milliman Medical Index has reported that the cost of healthcare for a family of four has reached $30,000 per year.[15] This excessive expenditure siphons financial resources that citizens rely on to keep their children in school, start businesses, or build a nest egg for retirement.

We are already seeing the detrimental effects of the unsustainable cost of the healthcare system. Over half of the country's personal bankruptcies in 2019 were due to surprise medical bills. Nationally, we spend $11,172 per person on medical expenses.[55]

On the world stage, these expenditure statistics are far from normal. The World Bank Group reports that average annual healthcare spending among all nations is approximately $1,100 per person. This average is roughly a 10th of the United States' annual healthcare expenditure of $11,000 per person. Moreover, when comparing developed nations, not only do other wealthy nations spend about half the amount that our nation spends, but their healthcare delivery systems also produce more favorable outcomes, including higher life expectancies and lower rates of chronic conditions.

This disproportionate healthcare spending places an unprecedented financial burden on citizens. In the previous section, we discussed how employers and government entities became the primary payers for American healthcare. But even after these parties pay their due portions, citizens are left with unaffordable medical bills. Consumers of American healthcare pay the highest out-of-pocket costs among all nations. These expenses include health insurance deductibles, copayments, coinsurance and all other hidden or unhidden expenses.

For example, at $4,092 per person, the U.S. out-of-pocket healthcare spending is more than five times that of Canada, the second highest spender.[57] In Sweden and Norway, out-of-pocket spending amounts to less than $100 per capita. And generally, as a share of total spending, out-of-pocket spending in the U.S. (around 40%) is significantly more than in any other country (about 0.3%–15%). In addition, financial resources that employers could use to raise wages for employees, provide retirement benefits, and create more jobs are instead siphoned into paying for medical care that, when compared on the world stage, produces results that are less than admirable.

The figure below compares GDP per capita and healthcare spending per capita for the United States and similar nations in 2019.[56] GDP per capita, or per person, is a measure of the size of the nation's economy, in proportion to the size of the nation's population. This is plotted on the horizontal axis. Healthcare spending per capita, or per person, is a measure of the average number of dollars spent on medical care for each person in the nation. This is plotted on the vertical axis. Across this figure, the drawn line demonstrates that, for most nations, as GDP per capita increases, the amount spent on healthcare for each citizen also increases proportionally. However, circled in black is a single, outlier nation that lies modestly in the center of the range of GDPs per capita, yet towers dramatically over its peers in healthcare expense: the

United States. The message is clear: our nation is spending above its means on healthcare!

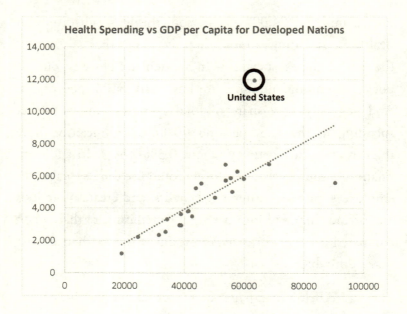

CHAPTER 2

# A MISPRICED HEALTHCARE WITH POOR HEALTH OUTCOMES

Even with its extravagant price tag, the American healthcare system trails in quality of health outcomes when compared to other nations. The starkest difference can be seen by comparing life expectancies between nations. Throughout the 20th century, as healthcare technology and clinical medicine advanced, developed nations experienced an upward trend in the average lifespans of their citizens. However, not all countries improved in this measure equally: among the 10 wealthiest nations in the world, the United States spends nearly twice as much as each of the other nations, but has the lowest life expectancy.[57]

The graph below plots life expectancy and medical spending by various countries. Most nations experience a proportional increase in life expectancy with an increased amount of per capita healthcare spending, with one exception: the United States. As we see, our nation spends about $11,000 with an average life expectancy of 79.7 years. In comparison, Iceland only pays $3,305 yet their people are averaging a lifespan of 82.9 years.

## United States vs. Other Countries

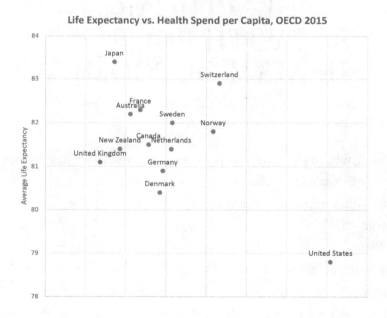

Moreover, while our nation benefits from medical innovation and advanced technology, researchers have shown that this medical advancement does not yield an increase in cost efficiency nor quality of life.[56]

When reviewing preventive services practiced by wealthy nations around the world, we can see that the U.S. has the highest rate of breast cancer and prostate screening among women and men ages 50 to 69 years old. But even after these impressive preventive measures, we are met with the contradicting statistic that states that the U.S. has the highest number of hospitalizations from preventable diseases as well as the highest rate of preventable death. Americans visit the doctor less than citizens of similar countries, which contributes to the shortened life expectancy and decrease in quality of life. At the same time, Americans opt for more expensive technologies to mitigate and diagnose diseases once they are found. Equipment like MRIs and specialized procedures like hip replacements are more popular in the United States, which contribute to an elevated price, although a large body of evidence has demonstrated that these expensive procedures do not lead to better health outcomes. From this information we can conclude that, even though our hospital-based healthcare system performs these expensive and excessive preventive measures more frequently than other wealthy nations, these measures ultimately do not contribute positively to an American's quality of life. Instead, they outrageously raise healthcare costs.

The table below shows healthcare spending per capita, stratified by age group, for the United States as well as similar nations. Nations generally spend more per capita on healthcare for the >65-year-old demographic than any other age group. This phenomenon is attributable to a greater need for medical care as citizens age. However, as shown in the table, the United States spends over 200% more than the average amount for its European counterparts on this demographic.134 And while there is a large disparity in healthcare spending for this cohort, the situation is even more bleak when taken in the context of the United States' healthcare outcomes.

**Per capita health expenditure by Age Group and Country**

| Country | 0-19 | 20-64 | >65 |
| --- | --- | --- | --- |
| United States | 4097 | 8161 | 24655 |
| Australia | 2525 | 3771 | 13316 |
| Canada | 2147 | 3366 | 11773 |
| Germany | 2448 | 3630 | 12442 |
| Netherlands | 2115 | 3763 | 12285 |
| Japan | 1711 | 2822 | 9972 |
| Switzerland | 2530 | 5166 | 16778 |
| United Kingdom | 1686 | 2705 | 9584 |
| Mean (SD) | 2166 (334) | 3603 (753) | 12309 (2213) |

Finally, although Americans spend more on their healthcare than any other nation, they are unable to access healthcare services at an equal or greater level than other leading nations. This is a recurring pattern seen in many areas of healthcare: though we spend twice as much as other nations, the U.S. underperforms when comparing positive health outcomes.

## Escalation of Chronic Conditions

The global distribution of chronic conditions also paints a dismal picture for the United States. As defined by the CDC, chronic conditions are "conditions that last one year or more and require ongoing medical attention or limit activities of daily living or both."[59] The United States has the highest rate of chronic medical conditions among comparable nations. For example, obesity in the U.S. is two times higher than average among the Organization for Economic Co-operation and Development (OECD), a collective of nations throughout the globe. Six out of ten Americans have at least one chronic condition, and four out of ten have two or more.[59] So, in addition to living shorter lifespans, American citizens also experience lesser quality of life that accompanies chronic conditions, when compared to other wealthy countries.

A significant body of research, as well as the events of the COVID-19 pandemic, has demonstrated that these chronic medical conditions impede many aspects of daily life and can even lead to death. In order to combat these ailments, and ameliorate the adverse effects they have on our healthcare system as a whole, we must first discuss the most common and detrimental conditions.

We previously discussed that citizens of advanced age require more medical care than other age groups and; therefore, cause a greater amount of national healthcare spending. The increased need of medical services for this age group is attributable to an increased prevalence of chronic conditions within the cohort. However, even though the elderly generally have more chronic conditions, American citizens of advanced age have a disproportionately elevated prevalence of chronic conditions when compared to citizens of similar age in other nations.

By far, the greatest risk factor contributing to the burden of chronic disease in the United States is obesity. Obesity affects one of five children and over two of five adults, and puts people at risk of other chronic diseases such as diabetes, heart disease, and some cancers.[60] Over a quarter of all American citizens between the ages 17 and 24 cannot join the military due to an unhealthy weight. Moreover, from a financial perspective, obesity costs the U.S. healthcare system over $150 billion per year.

Diabetes is also a significant and prevalent chronic condition.[61] More than 34 million Americans are diabetic. Another 88 million adults are prediabetic, which indicates a great risk of becoming diabetic. Importantly, there are two major types of diabetes: Type 1 and Type 2. While Type 1 Diabetes is not preventable, a host of lifestyle factors can mitigate, prevent, and sometimes even reverse Type 2 Diabetes. Diabetes affects almost every organ in the body and contributes to decreased quality of life and lifespan. Without vigilant management, this chronic condition can cause serious complications including heart disease, kidney failure, blindness, devastating blood infections, and loss of limbs.

Another significant set of chronic conditions is cardiovascular disease. Cardiovascular, or heart, disease is the leading cause of death for all Americans, affecting people of all sexes and ethnic backgrounds. It is rare to find a family unaffected by this nationally pervasive condition. High blood pressure, cholesterol, and smoking are among the most predictive risk factors for heart disease. Several other medical conditions and lifestyle choices can also elevate one's risk for heart disease, including diabetes, obesity, unhealthy diet, physical inactivity, and excessive alcohol use. Between 1996 and 2016, spending on adult care for cardiovascular disease increased by >$100 billion, which reflects an increasing strain on our healthcare system principally from heart disease. Nearly 80 years of research has demonstrated that we may prevent heart diseases by reducing the presence of modifiable risk factors in individuals. In addition, research has shown that population-level interventions that address the risk factors for cardiovascular disease appear to be effective and efficient.[17] Despite this, the evidence suggests that the preponderance of resources are still spent on treating the disease <u>after</u> establishment, instead of preventing it in the first place.

Cancer is another devastating set of chronic conditions. As the second leading cause of death in the U.S., cancer is one of the costliest health conditions that threaten the life and well-being of our nation. Most cancer risk factors and protective factors are initially identified in epidemiology studies. In these studies, scientists look at large groups of people and compare those who develop cancer with those who don't. These studies have demonstrated that the people who develop cancer are more or less likely to behave in certain ways or to be exposed to certain substances than those who do not develop cancer.

Risk factors for cancer include: age, alcohol, carcinogens, chronic inflammation, diet, hormones, immunosuppression, infectious agents, obesity, radiation, sunlight, and tobacco. Although some of these risk factors can be avoided, others—like aging—cannot. Consequently, risk reduction strategies have had mixed results in cancer. Success is seen in some strategies such as screening for precursors of cervical cancer in women and identifying active biomarkers including PSA for prostate cancer in men. However, undesirable results have been seen in large-scale efforts such as mammography for detection of early breast cancer, total body imaging strategies, and many other measures. These initiatives are the subject of ongoing evaluations by professional and peer-reviewed organizations such as the U.S. Preventive Services Task Force (www.uspreventiveservicestaskforce.org/uspstf/). Without a doubt, the effectiveness of our fight against cancer relies heavily on the number of resources our healthcare system can apportion to its prevention. Unfortunately, the majority of resources devoted to cancer are spent on treating and managing existing disease, not preventing it.

Another chronic condition affecting a large number of aging Americans is musculoskeletal problems. This group of conditions includes arthritis, pain, and other disabilities. Arthritis alone affects 55 million adults in the United States, which is about one in four people.[62] And, while arthritis is one of the most common chronic conditions, it is particularly impactful economically, as it is the leading cause of work disability and the leading cause of chronic pain.

Lastly, various mental health conditions constitute another type of chronic condition. Because the data concerning these issues is so alarming, both in older and younger generations, it would truly require an entire section to thoroughly discuss. Mental illnesses such as Alzheimer's disease and depression are increasingly devastating the quality of life of American citizens. Alzheimer's, a type of dementia, affects about six million Americans. This condition is the sixth leading cause of death among all adults and the fifth leading cause of death of those 65 years old and older.[63] Depression also affects a large portion of people in the United States, including nearly two million children.[64] Roughly 35 million Americans have diabetes, and they are two to three times more likely to develop depression than people without diabetes. The disease has also contributed to escalating suicide rates and severity of the opioid crisis, as afflicted individuals search for ways to cope.

The prevalence of these chronic conditions is steadily increasing, and this creates a destructive trend for the health of our nation as the 21st century unfolds. As exemplified by the total economic cost of obesity, chronic conditions are a major cause of excessive health expenses. In 2016, the total cost for direct treatment of chronic conditions in America totaled $1.1 trillion, which is equivalent to nearly 6% of the nation's GDP.[65]

**As we explore the results produced by our expensive healthcare system, one conclusion becomes clear: U.S. healthcare is a mispriced industry. We spend the most per capita but do not receive the best outcomes. This is analogous to a consumer paying a luxury price for a car, but receiving in exchange a gas-guzzling beater in dire need of repair.**

## Medical Errors Are the Third Leading Cause of Death in the U.S.

After having mostly eliminated fatal infectious diseases, the two prevailing causes of death in the U.S. remain cardiovascular disease (CVD) and cancer. Most alarmingly, however, is that following CVD and cancers, the third leading cause of death in the U.S. has become medical errors, as reliable reports have claimed that the annual number of deaths from medical errors is close to 440,000. This figure was cited in November 1999, when the U.S. Institute of Medicine (now National Academy of Medicine) issued a landmark report, entitled "To Err is Human: Building a Better Health System."[79] These figures indicate that we have unfortunately entered an era where overzealous delivery of medical services in the U.S. has started to create significant harm to the health of our nation, as these rates are significantly higher in the U.S. than in other developed countries such as Canada, Australia, New Zealand, Germany and the United Kingdom.[19] And though medical errors are often undocumented on death certificates as proximal causes of death, their cumulative impact has become large enough to raise significant concerns among academicians.[20] Such unnecessary harm runs counter to the intentions of medical services that are expected to improve health, not harm it, and therefore demonstrates an underlying misalignment of intent in the delivery of medical care. We will explore this topic further in a later chapter.

CHAPTER 3

# A HOSPITAL-BASED SICK CARE SYSTEM BENEFITING FROM SICKNESS OF THE POPULATION

The development of our healthcare system in the 20th century has left our nation with a multiple-provider healthcare delivery system featuring nearly 5,000 hospitals that exert primary control over the delivery of medical services. These hospitals have primarily become large financial institutions that employ most doctors, nurses, and other medical personnel; own outpatient surgeries, laboratories, and pharmaceutical services; and control other key components of the healthcare delivery system. The core business model of these hospitals is to provide services of all those components to the sick, while profiting from those services like any other large financial institution. For this reason, it is more accurate to describe our hospital-centered delivery system as a "hospital-based sick care system."

These hospitals, which were once charity houses established by various philanthropic and community supporters, have now turned into multibillion-dollar financial institutions, who follow the same playbook of any other for-profit multibillion-dollar organization.

Much has been written on this topic. Elisabeth Rosenthal, MD, a physician, reporter, and editor-in-chief of *Kaiser Health News* explains that these institutions, "[have] stopped focusing on health or even science [and instead focus] more or less single-mindedly to its own profits."[49] She eloquently reports on this matter both in her book, *An American Sickness*,[49] and her *New York Times* series published in 2014–2015, "Paying Till It Hurts."[133] Citing research and anecdotes, Dr. Rosenthal describes experiences where hospitals have billed for services that were never provided, or what she calls the "service of medicine and money." She explains that hospital bills are the most common cause of personal bankruptcy in America and that the Affordable Care Act did not significantly alter this trend. Further, following hospitalization, the income, credit worthiness, and net worth of hospitalized individuals and their families often decline by a significant margin.

To better understand the extent of the problem, let's review the ownership of hospitals, which can be divided into categories of state/local government-owned, nonprofit, and for-profit. This categorization yields the following national distribution:[50]

| Hospital Ownership | State/Local Government | Nonprofit | For-Profit | Total |
|---|---|---|---|---|
| United States | 18.7% | 57.3% | 24% | 100% |

Nonprofit hospitals comprise the majority of hospitals in the nation. Among these hospitals are: hospital systems that are owned and run by religious groups (Ascension, Catholic Health Initiatives); community or employer-based hospital systems (Trinity, Dignity, Sutter); and major academic medical centers that produce many billions in revenue annually (Mayo Clinic, Cleveland Clinic, University of Pittsburgh Medical Center).

The following list shows the nonprofit hospital systems ordered by the number of hospitals in each system:

Nonprofit Hospital Systems[51]

1. Ascension (St. Louis, MO) — 76
2. Trinity Health (Livonia, MI) — 45
3. Kaiser Permanente (Oakland, CA) — 37
4. Dignity Health (San Francisco, CA) — 36
5. Catholic Health Initiatives (Englewood, CO) — 33
6. AdventHealth (Winter Park, FL) — 31

7. Sutter Health (Sacramento, CA) — 26
8. Providence (Renton, WA) — 26
9. Northwell Health (Great Neck, NY) — 21
10. Banner Health (Phoenix, AZ) — 20
11. Baylor Scott & White Health (Dallas, TX) — 19
12. CHRISTUS Health (Irving, TX) — 19
13. SSM Health (St. Louis, MO) — 18
14. Intermountain Healthcare (Salt Lake City, UT) — 17
15. Mercy Health (Cincinnati, OH) — 17
16. New York-Presbyterian Healthcare System (New York City, NY) — 17
17. Adventist Health (Roseville, CA) — 16
18. UPMC (Pittsburgh, PA) — 16
19. UnityPoint Health (Des Moines, IA) — 15
20. Hospital Sisters Health System (Springfield, IL) — 14
21. Mercy (Chesterfield, MO) — 14
22. Texas Health Resources (Arlington, TX) — 14
23. Aurora Health Care (Milwaukee, WI) — 13
24. Baptist Memorial Health Care (Memphis, TN) — 13
25. Franciscan Alliance (Mishawaka, IN) — 13
26. Providence Saint Joseph (Orange, CA) — 13
27. Carolinas HealthCare System (Charlotte, NC) — 12
28. Sentara Healthcare (Norfolk, VA) — 12

29. Bon Secours Health System (Marriottsville, MD) — 11
30. Mayo Clinic Health System (Rochester, MN) — 11
31. Novant Health (Winston-Salem, NC) — 10
32. East Texas Medical Center Regional Healthcare System (Tyler, TX) — 7

The above hospitals are recognized as nonprofit entities. Their nonprofit status protects their income from taxes. However, the distinction between nonprofit and for-profit hospitals is grossly deceiving: both types of hospitals follow similar financial principles and function under the principle of "no margin, no mission." The only real difference is that nonprofit hospitals are expected to provide community services in lieu of paying taxes. Interestingly, research indicates that the majority of lawsuits against customers unable to pay their hospital bills originate from nonprofit hospitals, who are supposed to serve their communities.

The following list shows the list of for-profit hospital systems ordered by the number of hospitals in each system as of 2020:[51]

1. Community Health Systems —188
2. HCA Healthcare — 166
3. Tenet Healthcare (Dallas, TX) — 74
4. LifePoint Health (Brentwood, TN) — 56
5. Prime Healthcare (Ontario, CA) — 32
6. Universal Health Services (King of Prussia, PA) — 28
7. IASIS Healthcare (Franklin, TN) — 18

8. Ardent Health Services (Nashville, TN) — 12
9. Capella Healthcare (Franklin, TN) — 9
10. Steward Health Care (Boston, MA) — 9
11. National Surgical Hospitals (Chicago, IL) — 8

In 2019 a consumer advocacy group named OpenTheBooks studied revenues and asset growth for the top 82 nonprofit hospitals in the nation.[52] They reported that in 2018, patients spent roughly one out of every seven U.S. healthcare dollars on these healthcare systems. Many are household names: the Mayo Clinic, Cleveland Clinic, Kaiser Family Foundation, Dignity Health, and Partners HealthCare.

Despite the group's recognition as nonprofit entities, this report showed that the top 82 nonprofit medical providers are making big money.[52] In 2018, their combined net assets increased from $164.2 billion to $203.1 billion—that's 23.6% growth. Meanwhile, their executives are highly compensated. That year, the Banner Health President and CEO earned $21.6 million, and their Executive Vice President and CAO made $12 million. Top executives at Memorial Hermann Health System, Kaiser Permanente, Ascension, Advocate Health Care, and Northwestern Memorial made between $10 million and $18 million per year.

The researchers compared this growth to that of the five largest publicly traded for-profit hospital systems in the nation. These five corporations had $96 billion in revenue in 2018 with net asset growth of $600 million, representing an increase in assets from $40.1 billion to $40.7 billion year-over-year

(1.5% increase). Despite their for-profit status, these hospital systems trail in profitability and growth compared to their nonprofit counterparts.

Another alarming trend characterizing the hospital-based sick care system is that over the past two to three decades, these hospital systems have significantly consolidated into larger, multibillion-dollar systems that progressively extend their influence beyond both their home locations as well as the traditional role of hospitals in providing medical care. To name a few, the Mayo Clinic Health System, the University of Pittsburgh Medical Center (UPMC), and the Cleveland Clinic now have locations in multiple states and have recently expanded internationally, with locations in many nations across the globe.

These consolidations are advertised as solutions to reduce waste and cost or to provide benefits to consumers. But a significant and growing body of research suggests that their result is the opposite. Since 2010, approximately 100 hospital systems have participated in mergers. These systems report a consequent reduction in cost of around 16%–30%; however, at the same time, prices to consumers have increased by 6%–19% compared to pre-merger/acquisition numbers.[23] As a result, between 2012 and 2018, revenues for the 10 largest hospital systems, which control 24% of national patient care revenues, increased by 82%. Interestingly, this marked increase in hospital revenue has accompanied a moderate decline in quality of care, as measured by patient experience, 30-day readmissions, and mortality rates!

The difference between growth of hospital revenue versus any other industry or organization is that the hospitals are not compensated in relation to outcomes they provide to the healthcare consumer (the patient), but instead they are paid for the services they provide. Further, hospitals are also not paid in proportion to their service to the communities that subsidize their tax-free status. As we will discuss in more detail later, in most cases hospitals are paid in relation to the frequency and complexity of medical services they provide. This is the so-called fee-for-service model. In this model, hospitals are incentivized to perform the most complex medical services as frequently as manageable.

In many cases, complex medical services do not go as expected, and may harm the recipient; this is known as a "medical complication" or "adverse event," or simply harm to the patient. Hospitals are not negatively financially impacted following medical complications. As a matter of fact, hospitals financially benefit from the complications they produce. The Sun Life Stop-Loss & Health Research Report recounts statistics that confirm this observation. Between 2017 and 2019, "live births with secondary complications" was the sixth highest medical expense in their cohort, for a total cost of $143 million per year. Their seventh highest expense was "complications of surgical and medical care," for $125 million per year. Trailing behind these types of complications was organ transplants, for $103 million per year.[53] Alarmingly, treating the unwanted effects of healthcare has cost more than life-saving organ transplants.

Adding to the detrimental role of hospitals as financial institutions is that, as the employers of doctors and other providers, hospital systems have authority over the operations and practices of caregivers. As a result, hospital systems have negatively influenced the "doctor-patient relationship" that is a sacred part of clinical practice. By introducing financial misalignments for their employed doctors in this relationship, hospital systems have influenced the clinical practice to "more is better," which has created a major source of medical waste and harm in the U.S. healthcare system.

The CMS' Office of the Actuary estimated that the total healthcare expense for the entire American healthcare system reached $3.81 trillion in 2019 and would increase to $4.01 trillion in 2020.[48] They also projected that by 2028, healthcare spending would reach $6.19 trillion. Accompanying this growth, the proportion of healthcare expenses attributable to the "hospital-based sick care system" will grow to more than $3 trillion annually. To put this in perspective, this figure is 600% more than the U.S. defense budget and equal to the entire federal budget in 2019.

CHAPTER 4

# GOVERNMENT COST-CUTTING TRIALS DON'T WORK

The Social Security Amendments signed into law by President Lyndon B. Johnson on July 30, 1965, created two initial government-sponsored healthcare insurance programs: Medicare, a health insurance program for the elderly; and Medicaid, a health insurance program for people with limited income.* Both programs were funded by a tax on the earnings of employees, matched by contributions by employers and administered by the CMS .†

During the sixth decade of its life, CMS has become the largest payer of the U.S. hospital-based sick care system. Enormous in size, they also play a unique role as a part of the Department of

Health and Human Services in that they represent the federal government within the healthcare system. This has granted CMS a great deal of financial and authority leverage, giving them significant influence in the market.

In addition to functioning as a payer for healthcare services, CMS also serves as a regulatory agency, revising its own payment models with the intention to create efficiency and reduce the burden of healthcare spending on the federal budget. Like several other federal agencies such as the Food and Drug Administration (FDA), Environmental Protection Agency (EPA), and Federal Aviation Agency (FAA), the mere creation of CMS has established itself as what is named as the "fourth branch of the government."‡

* Debate over the program actually began two decades earlier when President Harry S. Truman sent a message to Congress asking for legislation establishing a national health insurance plan. At that time, vocal opponents warned of the dangers of "socialized medicine." By the end of Truman's administration, he had backed off from a plan of universal coverage, but administrators in the Social Security system and others began to focus on the idea of a program aimed at insuring Social Security beneficiaries whose numbers and needs were growing.

† Center(s) for Medicare & Medicaid Services is technically not one "Center" because it is distributed throughout eight different regions of CMS. However, the Centers function together as one Center, under the authority of the Secretary of Human and Health Services.

‡ The fourth branch of government is referred to as agencies that have the combined authorities of legislation, punishment, and execution within governmental functions that were never imagined by the Founding Fathers of the United States.

Beyond and above its numerous functions, CMS has been the federal government's apparatus for implementation in two primary directions: a) expansion of coverage for increasing numbers of Americans; and b) attempts to lower the escalating cost of healthcare. Herein, we briefly review the highlights of these two directions:

## 1. *Expansion of coverage of healthcare services:*

Over the past 57 years, multiple layers have been added to government-sponsored healthcare coverage with the goal of improving healthcare access for Americans. These expansions include: 1) Children Health Insurance Program (CHIP); 2) a basic benefit package for Medicare; 3) various health insurance reforms in the Clinton era;[69,70,71] 4) the Medicare Advantage Plan (also known as Medicare Part C);[72] 5) President Bush's Medicare Part D Prescription Drug Plans;[71] and, most extensively, 6) the Patient Protection and Affordable Care Act (also known as Obamacare)[73] in 2010.

## 2. *Attempts in lowering the cost of healthcare:*

Many other initiatives sought by CMS aimed to control or reduce total healthcare cost. These initiatives were meant to counteract cost expansion as the initiatives discussed in the section above increased the availability of healthcare to Americans. This issue of reducing cost, however, has proved more difficult to solve, and every administration since President Carter has presented some idea for cost containment. Diagnosis-Related Groups (DRGs)[66] were instituted to standardize payment for inpatient care. Relative Value Units (RVUs) were created and tied to different diagnoses and procedure codes (ICD and CPT) in an attempt to contain the cost, or at least measure a provider's value-based care. Finally, the Centers for Medicare & Medicaid Innovation (CMMI) was established by Congress in 2010 to create a research and development branch within CMS with the purpose of identifying ways to improve healthcare quality and reduce cost. CMMI's work has led to the creation of a number of "value-based programs" since its inception, however, concrete cost containment results have yet to be seen. We will review some of these initiatives later in Part IV of this book.

Despite various CMS initiatives, the escalating cost of healthcare is nearly daily news. Below are key findings from a Kaiser Family Foundation research finding in 2018:[24]

- In 2018, Medicare benefit payments totaled $731 billion, up from $462 billion in 2008.
- Medicare spending was 15% of total federal spending in 2018, and is projected to rise to 18% by 2029.
- Based on the latest projections in the 2019 Medicare Trustees report, the Medicare Hospital Insurance (Part A) trust fund is projected to be depleted in 2026, the same as the 2018 projection.

The alarming fact is that none of CMS' attempts have been able to reduce the cost nor control it to a level that is compatible with inflation or any other leading market indicators. So, it appears the government has succeeded in expanding healthcare access to more Americans but has not been able to control the cost or create efficiency. Increasing access has proven to merely create more excess.

The gap between accomplishments of these two directions by the government in healthcare perhaps presents the strongest argument against establishing a single-payer system in the United States. Expansion of government-sponsored healthcare to everyone without creating the needed efficiency will simply balloon the cost beyond the capacity of any governmental budget, and invariably some method of rationing must be applied, as Soviet-like era enterprises had to do! As Milton Friedman said, "Legislation cannot repeal the non-legislated law of demand and supply."

From the scientific angle, the strongest reason (in our opinion) for the failure of nearly 50 years of cost-cutting attempts is that none of those attempts address the fundamental pathophysiology of the sickness of our healthcare identified in this book. A wasteful healthcare system does not differentiate between government-sponsored payer and non-government payer, as a gas-guzzler car is passenger-agnostic too! An inefficient system will not become more efficient or function differently simply because the federal government is in the driver's seat. It is irrelevant who is riding a gas-guzzler: it will function wastefully and inefficiently for all of its passengers!

# PART III
## OUR HEALTHCARE SYSTEM IS SICK WITH WASTE! MOST AMERICANS AGREE

USA Today [74] published an alarming image on its front page in February 2020, which stated: "Voters actually agree: Our system is sick". According to this image, 92% of Americans were not satisfied with the healthcare system. For context, this publication occurred at the start of the COVID-19 pandemic and during one of the most politically contentious presidential elections, where Americans were deeply divided on many issues including solutions for healthcare. Nevertheless, they agreed overwhelmingly on one topic: the U.S. Healthcare system is sick and needs to change!

So, what are the root causes of this system's sickness?

CHAPTER 1

# ABUNDANCE OF WASTE: THE PRIMARY SIGN OF SICKNESS IN HEALTHCARE

A major contributor to the growing expense of our healthcare system is the waste that the hospital-based sick care system generates each year. The evidence of waste is widely recognized partly thanks to CMS, which has the ability to track billing and spending patterns across the country. Perhaps the initial credit should be given to Dr. John Wennberg,[77] emeritus professor and founder of the Dartmouth Institute of Healthcare, who started tracking the "unwanted variations in the healthcare industry" by following spending for the Medicare beneficiaries as early as the 1970s. He discovered that in his hometown, children had a 20% chance of having their tonsils removed, but in the town just next door, the likelihood of a tonsillectomy was 60%. This discovery propelled the rest of Dr. Wennberg's career, and his research has expanded to other like-minded scientists and researchers across the country who found that "30% of the services for Medicare beneficiaries could be eliminated without any impact on the outcomes." [74]

A landmark publication by Donald Berwick and Andrew Hackbarth in *Health Affairs* summarizes data suggesting that nearly 47% of total spending on healthcare in the United States is wasteful, consisting of services that do not generate positive health outcomes for patients.[75]

| Source of Waste | Estimated Annual Cost to Medicare and Medicaid (Billion USD) | Estimated Annual Cost to US Healthcare System (Billion USD) |
|---|---|---|
| Failures of care delivery | 45 | 154 |
| Failures of care coordination | 39 | 45 |
| Overtreatment (Unnecessary Care) | 87 | 226 |
| Administrative complexity | 56 | 389 |
| Pricing failures | 77 | 178 |
| Fraud and Abuse | 98 | 272 |
| Total | 402 | 1263 |
| % Of Total Spending | | 47% |

The sources of waste in healthcare can be categorized into three major sources:

## *Dysfunctional Access and Unnecessary Care*

The first source of waste is dysfunctional access to care that manifests itself at several layers of interaction between the consumer (patient) and the provider (doctors and hospitals).

Population-based data indicates that >90% of a person's needs fall within the scope of primary care, and less than 3% are needs within specialty or advanced hospital care.[135] However, due to the misaligned compensation scheme in the U.S. healthcare system that rewards expensive, complex services for providers, there is a significant shortage of primary care providers and an overabundance of specialists in most markets. Further, access to primary care services (to address 90% of the needs of a population) is grossly dysfunctional. Dysfunction in delivering primary care encourages consumers to use more expensive means of meeting their needs, or ignore issues until they escalate. The data indicates that over half of ER visits address medical issues that can be handled by simple visits with a primary care provider and would cost a fraction of emergency room costs. Upper respiratory tract infections, various acute illnesses, pain management, and minor trauma are common among these issues. However, upon arrival to urgent cares or ERs, providers in those settings have little or no background with the patient and have to consider a whole host of possibilities. Therefore, they order and perform a variety of unnecessary tests and procedures. ERs must be related to a hospital in order to handle a continuum of care possibilities, so the cost of ER care is astronomically high. Absence of a proper system by which simple health concerns can be handled by simpler and lower-cost providers is at the heart of this type of waste. In France, which ranks as one of the higher quality healthcare systems, nurses and doctors often visit the patients at their homes for their primary health concerns. Dysfunctional access to a proper care system creates significant medical waste in the form of unnecessary or harmful tests and procedures that only generate revenue for the hospitals with little to no health benefit to the consumer. In the further degeneration of this dysfunctional system, a high percentage of new patient arrivals are admitted to the hospital inpatient setting, where hospitalist doctors order a laundry list of tests and consultations, followed by a flurry of specialists who further accelerate the spiral of unnecessary care, costs, and potential harms. Many investigative stories can be written about this spiral! Being a specialist in several hospitals, I encounter this source of waste on a daily basis. In a recent encounter, I noted a consultation for urology for a patient who had a "urine complaint"!

## *Pricing Variability*

The second source of waste is pricing variability for diagnostic or therapeutic procedures that can vary as high as 1,500% in every city or market. The cost of a diagnostic MRI or a CT scan may vary anywhere from $250 to $4,000 depending on the provider and whether it is performed in an independent facility or one affiliated with a hospital. Labs, outpatient procedures, and surgeries also have the same unpredictable variability. A recent addition to this source of waste is the practice of hospitals acquiring independent private practices, and then labeling those outpatient clinics as hospital facilities. This allows hospitals to add "facility" fees to all services provided by the newly employed doctors, even though their services did not charge for facility fees before they became employees of the hospitals. As an example, if the cost of visiting your ophthalmologist or cardiologist is $150 (average price of an established outpatient visit), once a hospital system acquires the practice, you will expect to see an additional line item on the bill for a $300 to $600 facility fee.

Furthermore, as we discussed in our description of the multiple-payer system, despite the fact that all hospitals and doctors provide the same level of service to their patients, they receive different payment amounts depending on the patient's insurance plan (Medicare, Medicaid, or private). Imagine this scheme playing out in any other industry: to pay a different price for cars, houses, or food depending on who you work for or what type of credit card you have! The primary concern of this variability is that, on most occasions, the consumer has no idea of the cost of care until the care is rendered. In healthcare, unlike any other industry, the consumer receives their bill long after she has received the service. First, the consumer receives a notice in the mail that very much looks like a bill, but in big print says, "this is not a bill." This is the notice to inform the consumer about how much the hospital/doctor is going to charge the payer. Depending on what type of insurance the consumer has, she will be responsible for the "balance of the bill," or the remainder of the billed amount after the payer pays. Recognizing this source of waste, President Trump issued Executive Order 13877 on June 24, 2019 entitled "Improving Price and Quality Transparency in American Healthcare to Put Patients First." This executive order mandates price transparency across the provider sector.[76] On January 1, 2022, different parts of the price transparency rules went into effect. The triumvirate (Hospital Price Transparency Rule, Transparency in Coverage Rule, and the No Surprises Act) is easily confusing. The intention of this order and its three components is to inform consumers on the costs of healthcare services before receiving care and to prevent surprising and hidden billing practices by hospitals. It is too early to judge the impact of this law, but the hospital price transparency part of it, although having been in effect since January 1, 2021, has had no meaningful impact on this massive source of waste. For example, in January 2013 I performed a vasectomy on a patient in one of the hospitals in Northeast Ohio. During the post-op visit, my patient showed me the bill for this rather simple procedure: $9,000! Of this amount, my patient had to pay $1,000 out-of-pocket. The total price of doing a vasectomy in any independent doctor's office or Planned Parenthood clinic is approximately $500. Having had this rather embarrassing experience with my patient in 2013, as soon as the law went into effect in January of 2021, I did a search on the website of the same hospital. The site listed the price for a vasectomy as $8,000 for uninsured patients and $6,000 for insured patients. This short exercise was yet another confirmation that little gain can be made by top-down government rules and regulations, regardless of political alignment.

## Surprise and Hidden Billing Practices

The third source of waste takes the form of operational, administrative fraud that generates hundreds of billions of dollars of wasteful spending annually. The blame of this waste is equally shared between the hospitals and insurance companies who are continuously engaged in a push and pull game to increase their part of revenue to the detriment of the consumer. This pull and push has resulted in establishment of compounding opaque medical pricing strategies that have equal opaque billing practices in between the payers and providers. Starting with the Reagan administration, CMS has led the development of several coding systems that govern the level of payment for the healthcare services that hospitals and doctors provide to their customers/patients. Diagnostic related groups (DRGs), Current Procedural Terminology (CPT), International Classifications of Diseases (ICD), and Relative Value Units (RVUs) are all parts of a convoluted payment system that is used to report medical, surgical, and diagnostic procedures and services to entities such as hospitals, physicians, and health insurance companies. As a result, hospitals, doctors, and insurance companies are involved in a never-ending process of "gaming the system" including "upcoding," denials, out-of-network costs, or other games to increase their revenue from the rendered medical services. A significant part of resources in healthcare is spent on optimizing "billing practices" and their continuous manipulation. It is estimated that for every physician in the U.S. there is a minimum of $100,000 overhead expense for the process of billing. Additionally, it is estimated that these billing practices and the resultant fraud and abuse consume anywhere between 3% and 10% of national healthcare spending for a total cost of $200–$400 billion a year.[75]

Collectively, these sources of waste contribute to the ultimate cost of our healthcare system, making it the most expensive healthcare in the world! Many sources of waste aim to generate revenue for the multiple-payers and providers. Furthermore, much of this waste is masked from the consumer by the payer. Yet the party that ultimately foots the bill—the ultimate payer—is the consumer, through their forgone wages or paid taxes.

**These various forms of waste account for approximately one-third to one-half of all healthcare spending in the United States. This averages to roughly $1.5 trillion cumulative waste per year starting in 2018 and has grown to $2 trillion by 2020.**

CHAPTER 2

# THE HOSPITAL-BASED SICK CARE SYSTEM DRIVES THE WASTE

## AND INSURANCE COMPANIES PAY FOR IT

Numerous scientific and lay literature have thoroughly dissected the presence and increase in waste in the U.S. healthcare system, leaving any reader with the question: how can the wealthiest nation on Earth, equipped with the most advanced technologies and information, tolerate such waste in its largest industry?

As we discussed in a previous section, the United States' healthcare provider landscape has been altered over the past few decades. Larger hospital systems acquired smaller, community hospitals and, as a result, came to employ the majority of physicians in both primary care and specialist spheres. The purpose of this consolidation was to acquire control over healthcare referral channels that begin with primary care physicians (PCPs) and end with specialists. Most patients do not search out and meet directly with a specialist for their medical complaints, rather, they present these issues to generalists PCPs, who subsequently refer the patient to specialists. And while PCPs are not as directly profitable to their hospital systems as medical and surgical subspecialists are, more PCPs employed by a hospital system ultimately means more referrals to specialists, who are employed by the same hospital.

Once the patient is referred into a larger healthcare system, medical and surgical subspecialists perform diagnostic and therapeutic procedures, laboratory tests, inpatient admissions, and a host of other medical services that create "clinical volume" with associated revenue and help the hospital's financial goals. Over the past decade, increasing recruitment of "hospitalists" has added another layer to this vicious cycle. Hospitalists are the internal medicine-trained physicians whose job is to coordinate care for patients during their hospital stay. In practice, following their incentives of creating more clinical volume for the hospital, the hospitalist's role has turned into ordering many "consultations" with various specialists as soon as a patient is admitted to the hospital. So, in the outpatient setting, the primary care's role has turned into a referral machine for the hospitals; and in the inpatient setting, the hospitalists fill the same role. In the big picture, every physician working for a hospital is incentivized to feed the hospital mothership with more clinical volume in the form of more diagnostic tests, more consultations, more procedures, and more billable activities for the hospitals. This system and its misaligned incentives lack an incentive to slow down this process or change its course.

At the same time, through secret negotiations with insurance companies, each hospital and healthcare system secures contracts with various payment levels (prices) that are kept very close to their chest. Each hospital's Chief Financial Officer has three types of prices for the services of her hospital. The first one, called "billed charges," are bogus prices that each hospital generates fully knowing that no payer will pay those prices. The second set of prices are those the federal government/CMS pays (the Medicare rate). The third set is what the other insurance companies pay (commercial rate). The commercial rates are anywhere from 20% to 400% above Medicare rates. Hospitals love charging commercial rates and regularly compare their portion of bills paid at commercial versus Medicare rates as a key performance indicator called "payer mix."

The irony is that in this interaction between the hospitals as the seller/provider of services and insurance companies or government as the buyer of those services, the actual consumer is completely out of the loop. She has absolutely no choice but to pay for those prices by her forgone wages through her employer or taxes, and most irritatingly, is financially responsible for prices and ultimately receives the "balance bill." The balance bill is the remainder of the expenses that the third party has not paid, which becomes the obligation of the consumer. Two-thirds of people who file for bankruptcy cite balanced medical bills as a key contributor to their financial downfall.

CHAPTER 3

# WASTE LEADS TO GRAVE MEDICAL ERRORS

P.H., a neighbor of mine, was an 80-year-old man who would proudly go to our neighborhood gym every day. Conscious of his health though not experiencing any symptoms, he visited his doctor annually for routine check-ups, as many do. At one visit, his doctor informed him that he had atrial fibrillation, and though he had no clinical symptoms, his physician insisted that he take a blood thinner and a beta-blocker to reduce his risk of stroke. Trusting his doctor, P.H. complied.

Unbeknownst to P.H. were the side effects of his beta-blocker and blood thinner. Shortly after beginning his preventive regimen, P.H. stopped going to the gym because of fatigue resulting from the lower heart rate that follows taking beta blockers. A few weeks later, during a long-awaited trip to Paris with his wife, in his fatigue he missed a step on an escalator, fell, and sustained a large bleed (hematoma) in his leg. The injury required him to spend the rest of his vacation in a hospital in Paris before he was airlifted to the United States. P.H. stopped leaving his house for fear of falling and another bleed. Three months later, he was diagnosed with a gallbladder stone. Although the surgeon started to do the surgery laparoscopically (a lesser-invasive technique), he had to convert the operation to an open one (a more invasive technique), and close the much larger incision in a rush to prevent further bleeding. The next day, drainage of bowel content from the hastily closed wound was noted by the nurse. P.H. was taken back to the operating room for bowel resection and an enforced closure of his now large abdominal incision. These events required P.H. to stay in the Intensive Care Unit (ICU) for four weeks, followed by care in a rehab facility for two months, before returning home. He was never able to return to his favorite local gym again. A few months later, P.H. died from complications of depression.

This is a real-world case that demonstrates the intended and unintended consequences of unnecessary medical services, and it is rare to find a community that has not had similar experiences. Before his physician prescribed P.H. a blood thinner and beta blocker, P.H. did not experience any symptoms. Further, the doctor in his rushed visit failed to mention that P.H.'s active lifestyle is perhaps the best deterrent of a stroke! The start of these medications was intended to reduce by 20% the probability of stroke from a baseline of

0.78%–1.67% per year. Any active person with other major risk factors for stroke may accept that risk over the much higher risks of potential bleeds, fatigue, and lost opportunities that come with unintended consequences of unnecessary treatments.

Unfortunately, the case of P.H. is not an isolated or infrequent occurrence. Our hospital-based sick care system encourages a "more is better" approach as an essential part of its business model. Such an approach invariably leads to increased chances and prevalence of medical errors. Influential authors such as Dr. Atul Gawande have warned about the dangers of this mindset and harms of unnecessary medical care.[81]

The *Journal of American Medical Association* (JAMA) has recently created a series named "Less is More" to encourage physicians and thought leaders to submit publications that demonstrate the harms of healthcare's "more is better" approach prevalent in the current system. Articles in this series show how more stringent application of medical services have led to better health outcomes.[80] The published articles have included almost every common area of hospital services, ranging from surgeries for lower back pain, open or closed heart surgeries, and prostate surgeries, to other areas where the patients were subject to unnecessary care and procedures.

A 2016 study from Johns Hopkins suggests that medical errors are the third leading cause of death in the United States behind cardiovascular disease and cancer.[78] Over 250,000 people die every year as a result of these medical errors. Other reports have claimed that the number of deaths from medical errors is closer to 440,000. This figure was cited in November 1999, when the National Academy of Medicine issued a landmark report, entitled "To Err is Human: Building a Better Health System."[79] The report attracted attention to the alarming incidence of medical errors in the United States. For comparison, fewer than 50,000 people died of Alzheimer's disease and 17,000 died of illicit drug use in that same year.

Multiple theories attempt to describe the systemic causes of medical errors. From a systems design perspective, it is helpful to note that the value medical services can provide to a patient follows an inverted U-shaped curve. In an inverted U-shaped curve, the value that a service provides only increases to a limited extent (i.e., the left side of the upside-down "U"). After the amount of this service exceeds its natural benefit, the value that rendering more service provides will decrease (i.e., the right side of the upside-down "U") and may even become harmful. To put it simply, too little or too much of that service are both bad. This pattern is pervasive in healthcare: low blood pressure causes shock and death, while high blood pressure causes stroke and bleeding; underconsumption of food causes starvation, while overconsumption causes obesity. Meaningful inverted U-shaped patterns are found in several areas of social and biological sciences including economics, epidemiology, and medicine. The delivery of healthcare services in the U.S. also follows this pattern, and at present operates on the right side of the curve.

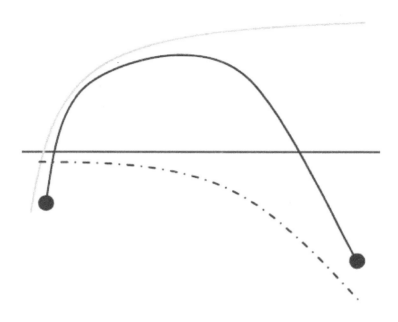

As evidence for this inverted U-shape pattern, healthcare is more costly and of lower quality in cities where hospitals merge into large health systems, and also where there are more hospitals and providers.[27] Markets such as Florida, California, New York, and Boston are the classic examples. Just as too few healthcare providers rendering an insufficient volume of healthcare services may leave some illnesses untreated, too many healthcare providers packed into large healthcare systems results in more waste and inferior health outcomes.

The high incidence of medical errors is best explained as a "system error," rather than the conscious fault of any individual provider. Any dysfunctional and/or misaligned system that seeks to maximize services rendered will also maximize the likelihood of error. As hospitals shifted in their roles from providing a place for recovery toward multibillion-dollar financial institutions, which focus on financial incentives by maximizing services provided to patients, this system maximizes the likelihood of error.

CHAPTER 4

# WASTE IS CLOAKED FROM THE CONSUMER
## EFFECTS OF THIRD-PARTY PAYERS

Tax exemption of healthcare coverage by employers following WWII, and later involvement of the federal government from 1965, introduced third-party payer intermediaries to pay large medical expenses for most Americans. At the same time, no third party is needed when we shop for other needs such as food, housing, or cars. As Milton Friedman, the Economic Nobel Laureate wrote, "Nobody spends somebody else's money as wisely or as frugally as he spends his own." The net effect of the third-party payment system has distanced and masked healthcare consumers from seeing the total amount of their money spent on healthcare, especially the waste. In their encounters with the healthcare system, most Americans only see the money they directly spend out-of-pocket, not the total cost of care. However, they do not realize that they ultimately pay for the TOTAL cost of medical expenses, not just their out-of-pocket portions, through their taxes (which fund government-sponsored coverage) and deducted wages (which are reduced by employers). In addition, there is an important distinction between health insurance and other forms of insurance such as car insurance. In all nonmedical examples of insurance (e.g., house or car), the consumers pay for maintenance and initial ownership fees directly, then pay a monthly premium for insurance on unexpected and catastrophic events such as fires or accidents. Healthcare insurance, however, pays for maintenance and unexpected events through a payment scheme that divides the total cost of care into premiums, coinsurance, deductibles, and copays. This method of payment has made the consumer only aware of "out-of-pocket" expenses such as deductibles or copays. The opacity of the true cost of care is further exacerbated for most Americans, who obtain their health insurance through employers, as most premiums are pre tax events deducted from their paycheck and are therefore invisible on bank statements. As a result, a knee replacement may in reality cost anywhere between $30,000 and $50,000 but the consumer only sees the minor part she pays directly, and she is therefore insensitive to the total cost.

Economists such as Milton Friedman reason that third-party payers are the root cause of over 50% of this expansion of total cost of care. Research[82] shows that between 2004 and 2019 the average annual cost of health insurance for employers increased from $7,300 to $14,500 dollars per employee, an increase of 100% for employers. During the same period, it increased from $2,660 to $6,015 dollars annually for employees, a 126% increase. As this research shows, the employees have not only paid the higher portion of the increase in premiums (126% increase for our part vs. 100% for the employer) but have also tolerated an increase in the premium paid by their employers, which ultimately comes out of the bottom line of the company and therefore employee wages.

**In summary, in the U.S. we spend the most per capita on healthcare, visit doctors less, and use more expensive and complex procedures, yet we suffer from higher rates of chronic conditions and lower life expectancies compared to other wealthy countries. In a nutshell, healthcare in the U.S. is an expensive and mispriced system. We pay 300%–500% more for a lower quality product.**

# PART IV
# THE ROOT CAUSE OF PERPETUAL WASTE: SYSTEMATIC MISALIGNMENTS

In any complex system, misalignments between its major components will yield dysfunction or poor results. After decades of studying and working in the dysfunctional healthcare system, I propose that the unintended results of our healthcare system, as discussed in previous chapters, are not the fault of any of its singular components, but are rather the results of systemic misalignments between those components as discussed below.

CHAPTER 1

# THE MISALIGNMENT BETWEEN FINANCIAL INCENTIVES OF PROVIDERS
## AND NEEDS OF HEALTHCARE CONSUMERS

The first step each would-be physician takes when becoming a doctor is to vow the Hippocratic Oath.[85] This is an oath to uphold the value of nonmaleficence, "First, do no harm"— a vow to protect the health of each patient. The first violation of this millenia-old principle is the concept of "fee-for-service." Doctors receive payments for each service they provide. This was not a major problem until hospitals started employing the doctors. Now, the doctors are the agents of hospitals and are rewarded financially in proportion to the number of healthcare services they provide, even if the services are not needed or even harmful. The phrase "pay for performance" describes how doctors are paid better for providing more sick care services. For centuries, patients have trusted doctors to provide services that treat their specific illness or maintain their health—and nothing more. However, the consolidation of hospital systems and the massively centralized employment of physicians by multibillion-dollar financial institutions has compromised this vow and eroded the underlying trust between the doctors and their patients. In its place, a new financial alignment has emerged between doctors and the hospitals that pay their salaries and provide "pay for performance" bonuses. In most hospitals, the physician's compensation is directly related to the clinical volume they generate. When we, as consumers of healthcare, are ill or need doctor services, we put our trust in the judgment and intentions of our doctors based on our common belief in the Hippocratic Oath. Unfortunately, our doctors, who are expected to be our agents, have instead become the agents of multibillion-dollar financial institutions known as hospitals. We might imagine an analogous situation. Consider if we relied on the good intentions of a car salesperson to sell us a car while prioritizing our lifestyles and budget over their sales records and commission. Our trust would simply be misplaced. One might interject that doctors and car salespeople differ greatly in professional ethical standards, but the significant growth in unnecessary care as prescribed by doctors, the warnings of medical professional organizations, and numerous other findings discussed previously have demonstrated the error in this axiom.

In response to the growing concern of physician's conflicts of interest and financial misalignments, professional physician groups have formed an organization called Choosing Wisely[87] that promotes constructive, serious dialogue between doctors and their patients to ensure that sick care services offered to patients are supported by evidence, remain free from harm, are truly necessary, and are not redundant with previous care. The very necessity for the establishment of such an organization attests to the prevalence of unnecessary health services in our hospital-based system and the presence of fundamental financial misalignments.

Based on real stories that are sometimes difficult to believe, Dr. Erika Schwartz warns patients of the harmful trends dominating the hospital-based sick care system in her book *Don't Let Your Doctor Kill You*.[86] In her book, she describes her experience as a young ER doctor in New York City, witnessing the rise of corporate medicine as competition for patients, money, influence, and accolades began to dominate the profession. Starting in the early 1990s, she started documenting her observations of how the incentives shifted toward "more is better" and away from positive health outcomes. As a result of common medical errors, many patients she observed left the hospital in poorer health than when they arrived. Eventually, she decided to compile her notes into a book. She states, "I was ready to expose the countless careless cases of mistakes I witnessed on a daily basis."[86] However, her publisher warned her against publishing her notes, suggesting that she was too idealistic and exaggerated the cases. Over the next three decades, she witnessed the same trends escalate until she finally decided to publish her book, which became a *New York Times* bestseller.

One can argue that the cumulative result of these financial misalignments is demonstrated in alarming evidence that medical errors and bodily harm from medical care have become the third leading cause of death in the U.S. Recent studies of medical errors have estimated errors may account for as many as 250,000 deaths annually in the United States. Error rates are significantly higher in the U.S. than in other developed countries such as Canada, Australia, New Zealand, Germany, and the United Kingdom.[83] These data suggest that misaligned financial incentives, resulting in healthcare waste and medical errors, are a significant source of mortality nationally.

## Primary Care as the Referral Machine for the Hospital-Based Sick Care System

Over the course of scientific development during the 20th century, doctors have branched out into a variety of specialties requiring training above and beyond medical school. This was a necessity following the rapid expansion of our understanding of human physiology and disease. Every graduate of an allopathic or osteopathic medical school can obtain a license to practice medicine pending completion of additional post-graduate training called "internships" or "residencies." Physicians who complete training in Family Medicine, Internal Medicine, or Pediatrics are categorized as "primary care" physicians (PCPs), while those who complete other types of training (which may be either medical or surgical training) such as neurology, nephrology, cardiology, urology, neurosurgery, and cardiac surgery are considered specialists. In an ideal world with an ideal healthcare system, a PCP's job would be to address the common health needs of an individual, while making sure that those needs do not escalate in complexity to require a specialist. For example, a physician should control a person's blood pressure by helping her reduce her weight, improve her diet, and make other lifestyle improvements. Such lifestyle modifications would prevent hypertension from causing further damage that would require the attention of a cardiologist, nephrologist, or vascular medicine specialist.

In this ideal scenario, PCPs would be agents of healthcare consumers, or patients, by working to maintain and improve the health of their patients, rather than being agents of the financial interests of hospitals. Furthermore, the same alignment would exist between a patient and her specialist, though this is admittedly more difficult since we know that a specialist's work only starts after a medical issue has escalated enough to require her level of expertise. Therefore, we can conclude that healthcare specialists are truly sick care doctors. The job of a heart surgeon is to fix a leaky valve, and the job of a urologist is to take out the kidney stone or relieve the obstruction. There is little incentive in prevention of those diseases for specialists. They are trained and paid to take care of medical conditions that have escalated to their level of expertise, not to prevent them.

The case should be very different for the primary care physician. PCPs should be interested and be rewarded for keeping a person healthy, preventing escalation of initial issues to more complex problems, helping their patients adopt positive changes in their lifestyles, and managing compliance with medications. Anything that they can do to keep their patients healthy should fall within the scope of primary care.

However, over the past 30 years, hospitals have realized the critical role of PCPs as the "gatekeeper" of patients. PCPs generally control which specialists patients see. To control patient referrals, hospital systems now understand that they must control the referral practices of PCPs. To do this, they must employ PCPs. In most large cities, the major hospital-based systems now employ the majority of PCPs to secure their "referral bases." They enforce referral practices by instituting compensation incentives that prevent or disincentivize PCPs from referring patients anywhere else, even if this would inconvenience the patient or would provide a different quality of care. These hospitals mandate that the PCPs send their patients to specialists who work for the same hospital system and encourage the PCPs to refer their patients to specialists as early as possible. Once the patient is referred, specialists generally run more tests and other expensive services than a PCP would. In this new alignment between the PCPs and the hospitals they work for, the PCPs are not rewarded by how well they maintain the health of their patients, but by their "productivity" defined as the number of patients they can see in an hour and how often they refer their patients for other services provided by hospitals, including labs, imaging, or referrals to specialists. In a nutshell, PCPs are compensated in proportion to how much "clinical volume" they generate! In internal communications of the hospitals, this strategy is referred to as "keepage," to increase and keep all the clinical volume within a single hospital system.

These efforts towards maximizing "keepage" have fundamentally changed the alignments between PCPs and the consumers of healthcare, and has caused further escalation of the cost of health care.[84] As its ultimate consequence, PCPs are no longer agents for the consumer, but rather a referral machine for the hospital-based sick care system.

It is important to note that in this discussion we are analyzing trends in evidence. There are exceptions to any rule, and there are individual PCPs out there who do their best to maintain their allegiance to the Hippocratic Oath. Though a minority, these physicians prioritize resolving the medical issues of their patients, instead of simply functioning as a referral machine for their hospital system.

If we attempt to imagine a PCP acting as a true agent for a healthcare consumer, we imagine a much different scenario from what is played out in hospitals today. The aligned PCP's role would be to keep a person in good health, working diligently to eliminate any need for hospitalization, short of uncontrollable traumas. The PCP would keep watch over factors influencing their patient's health with enough vigilance to notice an extra weight gain, increase in stress, or other lifestyle factors and health risks that could be modified. Upon noticing one such factor, the ideal PCP would intervene with advice or directed care far before a specialist consultation or hospitalization is needed.

This misalignment has recently received more attention. In an attempt to reverse it, a growing group of PCPs are adapting to a "Direct Primary Care" (DPC) model. Direct indicates direct payment to the PCP by the consumer of healthcare. With a direct contract between the PCP and a patient, the DPC model restores the traditional model of agency where the PCP works for the person and gets paid by them directly. In this model, a PCP receives membership fees from 400–500 individuals and becomes their concierge physician.[108] We will discuss the impact of DPC in the later chapters of this book.

In summary, today's healthcare delivery is structured such that it maximizes the financial metrics of a hospital-based sick care system, which benefits from our illness and not from our health. Our system has created a misalignment between the ideal intentions of doctors, their financial incentives, and the hospital systems that employ them. This misalignment profoundly influences the care that doctors provide, as well as the facilities, providers, and procedures they refer their patients to.

CHAPTER 2

# THE MISALIGNMENT BETWEEN THE PAYERS AND THE PROVIDERS

The goal of any "healthcare system" should be to keep the population it serves healthy and lower their illnesses. However, the hospital-based sick care system exhibits an inherent misalignment between their own financial interests and the health interests of their customers and their sponsors (employers that pay for over 200 million Americans and the federal government that pays for nearly 100 million Americans). Hospitals advertise that their mission is to improve the health of the population they serve, but this promise runs counter to the aims of their business models and financial interests, which rely on increasing clinical volume by increasing diagnostic and therapeutic services. Keeping people healthy would preclude hospitals from increasing their clinical volume. The more patients a hospital admits, the more procedures and surgeries they perform, the more revenue they ultimately generate, and better bonuses their management receives. Hospitals are not engaged in measuring the real indicators of health within their patient population. On the contrary, research indicates that in communities where bigger hospitals purchase smaller hospitals, quality of care decreases and prices increase.[27]

Realizing this significant misalignment, major payers including Medicare have advocated replacement of fee-for-service models with a new system of compensation for doctors and hospitals named "Value-Based Care" (VBC).[109] The idea of VBC is that the providers should be paid based on the healthcare value they deliver. However, this model does not clearly define whose values it intends to protect. Furthermore, unlike any other industry where consumers organically define value through their purchase preferences and feedback, the VBC model provides a definition of value from the sponsor's standpoint and not the consumers. The CMS site describes these types of programs as such, "These programs are part of our larger quality strategy to reform how healthcare is delivered and paid for."[138] Over the past decade, CMS and its Center for Innovation have launched a number of initiatives aimed toward improving the effectiveness of their value-based programs. The most recent program is "Accountable Care Organizations" (ACOs) or "Direct Contracting" (DC) schemes that reward doctors (mostly PCPs) for keeping their patients healthy. DC is a set of voluntary payment model options aimed at reducing expenditures and preserving or enhancing quality of care for Medicare beneficiaries. The effectiveness of these programs is yet to be determined.[132]

The financial interests of hospital systems fundamentally prevent their meaningful participation in improvement of population health, as their business interests are in contrast with maximizing health outcomes and reducing healthcare cost. The reality is that, like any profitable institution, hospitals function based on a set of financial goals and strategic plans that include delivering a positive margin. The problem is that there is no limit to the sick care services a hospital can deliver to a patient. In the current healthcare model, the seller dictates how much service the buyer needs. Healthcare is primarily delivered through nearly 5,000 hospitals that follow these misaligned incentives, so it is no wonder that healthcare costs have continued to escalate.[82]

CHAPTER 3

# THE MISALIGNMENT BETWEEN INTERMEDIARIES
## EXPLOSION OF UNNECESSARY CARE AND COST

As a nontaxable employment benefit initiated during WWII, and later under a number of other regulatory mandates, employers with 50 or more employees are obligated to provide healthcare benefits to their employees. Employer-sponsored healthcare benefits pay for medical expenses for more than 200 million Americans. The larger employers (more than 1,000 employees) self-insure their healthcare fiduciary responsibilities. However, smaller employers (under 500–1,000) buy insurance packages from insurance companies (this arrangement is called a fully insured employer). In the majority of cases, the "healthcare benefits" are packaged by a host of intermediaries known as brokers (or advisors and consultants). Brokers may either be independent contractors or indirect employees of insurance companies, and they function to package a bunch of healthcare benefits (hospitalizations, dental, vision, etc.) to sell them to employers. The interaction between the insurance companies who provide the insurance coverage and employers is mediated through several layers of brokers, including master general agents, general agents, master brokers, and final sales brokers. Each layer of brokership adds another middleman to the equation, who takes a portion of the premium paid by the employer as commission. The higher the premium, the more commission these brokers bring home.

The Affordable Care Act (ACA) has attempted to limit the proportion of premium dollars that are paid to the insurance companies and their chain of brokers to 20% of the total premium. In industry terms, this means that the "medical loss ratio" (dollars received in premiums versus dollars spent on healthcare expenses) must be kept above 80%. However, ACA did not cap the total amount of premiums collected; hence, creating another misalignment that incentivizes ever-increasing premiums. 20% of a $1,000 premium is much less attractive than 20% of a $10,000 premium for an insurance company that seeks to maximize revenue.

**As you may appreciate by now, the mere existence of the above-mentioned misalignments between 1) the doctors and their patients, 2) the hospitals and the payers, and**

3) the insurance companies and employers have created a variety of loopholes that enable healthcare waste to proliferate in the form of overutilization of medical services, price variability, administrative costs, and fraud. It is no wonder that these sources of waste contribute to nearly 50% of medical waste.[67]

# PART V
# CHANGES OF LIFE IN THE 21ST CENTURY THAT DEMAND CHANGE IN HEALTHCARE DELIVERY

CHAPTER 1

# DEMOCRATIZATION AND DEMONETIZATION OF HEALTH INFORMATION
## (DR. GOOGLE!)

When discussing medicine in the modern era, we must not ignore the elephant in the room: the impact of technology. Digitization, democratization, and demonetization of health information has spread like wildfire throughout the internet. Access to the internet through innovation and proliferation of cell phones, tablets, and personal computers has fundamentally altered the way that consumers, providers, and payers interact with our healthcare system.

From the consumer's perspective, the general American population has a new resource to address their many health-related questions, which does not accompany the many burdens associated with a doctor's appointment. Many people have taken advantage of this new resource by using "Dr. Google" as their new health consultant. In fact, according to the Pew Internet & American Life Project, about 59% of adults in America now turn to the internet with their health-related questions and concerns.[106] This method of access to health information has largely replaced traditional channels among newer generations, including Millennials (born between 1981–1996) and Gen Z (born between 1997–2012): two generations that have never lived without emails or internet access.

The democratization of health-related information has become more achievable through search engines like Google and other companies, who have created more accessible explanations, resources, and communities involving healthcare. This movement has led to more consumers participating in their own health, which is positive because it creates self-sufficiency and ownership in one's health and medical journey. Concurrently, the democratization of health information has created a bit of an awkward scenario; consumers now rely too much on Dr. Google, and consequently, try to self-manage their health issues without dialogue or engagement with their physicians. This is intended to avoid both the cost and burdens associated with access to the existing hospital-based sick care system.

Such ease of access to health and medical information in the midst of a misaligned healthcare system has the potential to create another layer of dysfunctionality. The integral component of the physician-patient relationship—the interpretation of medical information and health recommendations—has not yet been completely figured out in this new era of information democratization. This creates inaccurate interpretations of the information one obtains from using Dr. Google. For example, a study in 2016 found that Dr. Google and other websites that allow you to match experienced symptoms with potential diagnoses are only accurate about 34% of the time.[107]

In addition, a significant portion of personal health information is still "held hostage" in electronic medical records of the hospital-based sick care system. Even though providers hoped technological advancement and the digitization of healthcare information would lead to increased portability of patient health information, this hope has not yet been realized. Under the American Recovery and Reinvestment Act,[108] the government mandated the use of electronic medical records (EMRs). And even though EMRs have proliferated in use throughout the healthcare system, they, by and large, lack functionality for easily transferring consumer health information between different provider systems.

This lack of development is disappointing, especially compared to the developments made in other industries such as banking and finance. These industries have utilized the digital sphere to create seamless access and streamlined experiences for their consumers. However, the healthcare realm has not been able to develop similar programs. Patient health information continues to be siloed within the hospital-based sick care system. Initiatives in this sphere by major tech companies, like Google and Apple, have yet to provide access to our health information comparable to services they have created in other types of personal information like financial data.

CHAPTER 2

# TELEMEDICINE AND VIRTUAL DELIVERY OF CARE

Between the end of the 20th century and the beginning of the 21st century, American society experienced a huge expansion of technology. From cell phones to the internet, nearly every aspect of our lives seems to have become digitized, especially in the domains of communication, education, shopping, parenting, and beyond.

And with the digitization of our lives came the most personal part of our changing world: the democratization of knowledge as it relates to health. With greater access to information from the internet, access to health and medical knowledge is no longer limited to a few experts. People are able to adopt more autonomy when making decisions regarding their health and lives because they have access to more information. Even within a few hours of research, modern technology allows an individual to obtain and transfer important and personal medical information. While this might seem like a basic process, it was not until the last few decades that such communication between doctors, patients, businesses, and other important personnel was possible.

In 2018, surgeon, writer, and public health researcher Dr. Atul Gawande recounted in an article for *The New Yorker* the impact of digitization as experienced by physicians and other healthcare professionals.[110] He noted the resistance and hesitancy he and his fellow doctors felt towards implementing new technology into their day-to-day interactions with patients. The excessive time spent on the computer resulted in time-consuming paperwork after-hours and less face-to-face time with patients. But, he also acknowledged the enhanced communication and sharing of information, explaining how this advancement allowed him to "remotely check" his patient's vital signs and quickly receive test results from outside institutions.

The exponential expansion of the internet has also altered healthcare delivery, especially in how people involve their physicians in treating present symptoms. The term "Google it" has made its way into almost daily conversation as people try to solve their own ailments. It has infiltrated the educational vocabulary of medical students as they train for positions in healthcare, is present in residency programs as resident physicians hone their clinical expertise, and even shows up in the dialogues of attending physicians during day-to-day management of patients and their various health conditions. Google has asserted the claim that about 5% of the total daily searches are symptom related[112] and a study from 2019[113] found that 89% of people Google their medical concerns before asking their doctor.

On a generational level, some studies show that members of the Millennial and Generation Z generations more often turn to the internet to learn about their medical concerns rather than asking their doctors first. And sometimes they trust their own findings from places like Google or WebMD more than their physicians. One study conducted by Harmony Health IT in February 2021 found that 42% of participating Millennials had more faith in their online research than their doctor's advice.[114]

In the COVID-19 pandemic, social restrictions and concerns about spreading COVID-19 gave rise to a great expansion of telehealth, which as we can now understand was made possible by the advancements in cell phones and the internet. When CMS compared the last week of March in 2019 to the last week of March in 2020, they saw a 154% increase in the utilization of telehealth[115] for communication with their medical professionals. These days, an individual only needs access to her phone, tablet, or laptop and a stable connection to the internet in order to receive a diagnosis, referral, or prescription. Though technology for delivering telehealth had been developed and was in meager use before the COVID-19 lockdowns and social distancing measures, it was usually set aside for situations that demanded remote care. After the COVID-19 pandemic, however, telehealth has now been redefined as a routine option for the delivery of healthcare.

CHAPTER 3

# BIOMEDICAL TECHNOLOGY

It is impossible to discuss the full extent of recent advancements in medical technology in one single chapter or even one full book. Developments in medical science and the needs of our population are constantly evolving and reshaping how we deliver medicine and experience physician-patient interactions.

Nevertheless, one major development in health technology that has fundamentally changed our relationships with medicine and our bodies was the discovery of DNA and its structure. In 1953 James Watson and Francis Crick identified the double-helix structure of DNA, which opened the floodgates for the study of molecular biology, genetics, and our ability to manipulate sequences of DNA, for better or worse. This forever altered the trajectory of health sciences and healthcare.[116]

Among many discoveries that followed the discovery of DNA that specifically relates to the interest of this book is CRISPR technology, which is short for CRISPR-Cas9. This is a major technological advancement and a powerful tool for editing genomes. It provides the mechanism to cut or break DNA sequences and influence the cells that repair this break to develop in a new, specific way for a new, specific purpose. This advancement can potentially improve or correct genetic defects, and ultimately treat and prevent the spread of infectious diseases.

In 2019, CRISPR technology[117] saw its first success with two patients suffering from blood disorders. After their gene-editing treatment, one patient was healed of her pain and another no longer needed to receive blood transfusions to manage her hemoglobin levels.

Surgeries performed by robots have also seen significant growth within the last few years. In 2018, a report showed that robot assistance was used in 15.1% of all surgeries performed in the United States.[118] There are clear benefits to this mode of procedure. For example, robotic surgeries require smaller incisions, which result in less pain and scarring for the patient. Furthermore, this less invasive approach has also allowed patients to recover faster and spend less time in the hospital after their procedure. The surgeon also gains some benefits. While using robotic equipment, the doctor can achieve an enhanced visual field, make use of a robotic arm that rotates a full 360 degrees (unlike the physical limitations of human hands), and have better access to places that are difficult to reach.

Medical technological advancements have contributed to a greater quality and length of life for those who suffer from many of the diseases and cancers that have proven to be deadly to humans for centuries. For example, molecular technologies that target both healthy and diseased components of our cells and organs have become a routine element of diagnostic and therapeutic nuclear medicine, specifically in cancer patients. This type of therapy may include "blocking molecules" that can kill cancer cells or at least prevent them from growing and spreading. More recent developments have shown that this type of therapy might be less harmful, with fewer side effects, than other cancer treatments.

Perhaps the epitome of this technological advancement in communication and information sharing within medicine was the development of an mRNA vaccine for SARS-CoV-2, the COVID-19 virus. Under usual circumstances, vaccine development is a tedious journey that takes somewhere between 10–15 years to accomplish.[111] But, as we can all attest, 2020 was not a year of usual circumstances. In response, the Department of Health and Human Services developed a plan titled "Operation Warp Speed" to expedite vaccine innovation. The speed with which information regarding SARS-CoV-2 mRNA, and its vaccines, traveled is what allowed for the FDA to grant emergency use authorization for the COVID-19 vaccine. This ultimately minimized the timeframe for vaccine development and approval from over ten years to just a matter of months.

A host of other technological breakthroughs in medicine have improved patient care and the quality of work performed by doctors. For example, 3D printing has developed within the last five years to meet specific needs of each unique patient. While full organs have not been printed and implemented, doctors have successfully created and administered kidney cells and sheets of cardiac tissue to help their patients.

Augmented reality and virtual reality have also found their place outside of arcades and video games, and into the educational spaces of the healthcare industry.[119] Students are able to experience more realistic and cohesive models, and gain better access to elements of the human body that they could otherwise not conceptualize. Beyond medical school, virtual and augmented reality has also been used to help individuals overcome intense mental trauma.

Despite the excitement concerning various technological advancements, it is important to recognize that no single advancement may solve the systemic misalignments inherent in healthcare. As Milton Friedman states, "technological advancements in healthcare will only add to ballooning expenses and waste, as it has over the past several decades."[139] All advances in diagnostic and therapeutic technologies have worsened the unaffordability of American healthcare, in contrast to all other industries, where technological advancements have generally made services and products more affordable and accessible. For example, cell phones, televisions, airline transportation, ebooks, online shopping, and internet connectivity have all become more affordable and accessible as a result of technological advancement. In addition, this process of affordability and improved access has disrupted or abandoned the traditional modes of delivery of services and products, such as retail stores. Therefore, the systemic misalignments within the contemporary American healthcare system must be solved before we can truly harness the potential of these promising technological advancements.

Peter Diamandis, MD, a physician, engineer, and entrepreneur, summarizes the changes of the past two decades of various industries in the "6 D's" framework, which may serve as a lens and a roadmap to predict and benchmark future exponential growth of other industries.[120,121] This "6 D's" framework includes six states of innovation: Digitized, Democratized, Deceptive, Disruptive, Demonetized, and Dematerialized. The net effects of full implementation of "the 6 D's" in healthcare would transform a significant portion of healthcare delivery from its current status where most interactions are physical (visits to the doctor, doing various tests, or procedures) and are dictated by the providers site and time preferences, to a position where most interactions are done virtually and are delivered at the time and place preference of the consumer at a fraction of today's cost. Explosion of telemedicine solutions during the COVID-19 pandemic may give us an introductory window to a potential exponential growth in this industry where access to the most advanced healthcare can be achieved on one's mobile device. A summary of "the 6 D's" can be found in the appendix section of this book.

The scope of medical technology and its rapid advancement show no signs of slowing down, with the hope that the end result of this exponential growth will be an improvement in access, affordability, and higher quality of care.

CHAPTER 4

# ARTIFICIAL INTELLIGENCE

An entire book could be written on applications of artificial intelligence (AI) in healthcare. Use of healthcare data has been explored by a number of initiatives since EMRs have proliferated in healthcare. EMRs have facilitated the collection of an enormous volume of data. Processing data of this size is far beyond the normal capacity of humans, as traditional analytical techniques and databases only take us so far. Thus, AI is a promising field of study that aims to harvest insight from this overwhelming corpus of data. Large projects such as the well-known IBM Watson have explored using AI in medicine to put this insight to use.

To illustrate the use of artificial intelligence in healthcare, let's review a common process in traditional medicine. When a patient arrives at a clinic for a visit with a physician, they are generally greeted by a medical assistant who escorts them to an examination room and administers paperwork to collect data on patient demographics, diagnoses, and medications as they wait for the physician to arrive. While this interaction and data collection may be simple, it is both time consuming for the patient and requires physicians to hire office personnel. A solution involving AI would allow the patient to provide this information at her convenience, perhaps even before she enters the office. Furthermore, instead of a barrage of paperwork to fill out, AI would not only pre-populate questions from the patient's health record, but also filter questions down to only those relevant to the patient's health concerns.

Another common process in healthcare is reviewing labs or diagnostic tests. This set of processes really constitutes an entire industry within healthcare, as millions of labs are ordered every day. Generally, the healthcare provider collects a sample from the patient (blood, urine, or sputum for instance) before sending it off to a facility which conducts the tests. The result of the test is then assessed by a technician before the result is communicated to the physician's office. The physician's personnel may then either call the patient to discuss the results or request an appointment for further discussion. A solution that involves AI may be useful at multiple steps in this process. Firstly, assessing the results of tests is labor intensive and requires trained technicians; however, an AI construct may be trained to distinguish between "normal" and "abnormal" in an automated manner. Secondly, samples may often be contaminated, and AI models may be able to detect anomalous samples that greatly deviate from the norm. Thirdly, an elegant AI solution may enhance a physician's ability to communicate results with patients; for instance, patients may appreciate an AI construct that automatically communicates normal test results to them within an hour of completing the test, but forwards abnormal test results to the provider for their review. This type of solution allows for seamless, rapid communication between healthcare providers and their patients, and is even used in some COVID-19 testing facilities at present.

Finally, AI may be useful in processes that involve clinical decision-making. Many common decisions made by healthcare providers can be turned into algorithms, or standardized processes that consider a collection of input data and result in various output actions. In fact, much research has been conducted in every field to produce clinical diagnostic algorithms and clinical treatment algorithms for most complaints a patient can present. Let's consider the issue of blood sugar control in an insulin-dependent diabetic person. When the individual's blood sugar is uncontrolled, we must administer insulin; however, the amount of insulin we administer must be computed from both the patient's current blood sugar levels and the target levels established within physician-patient discussions. This need not be computed by the patient on the fly. We have seen that these types of solutions are susceptible to human error and even death. Instead, an elegant solution that involves AI may continuously monitor interstitial sugar, alert the patient when her sugar levels are elevated, and inform the patient on the appropriate corrective dose of insulin. This solution may go even further; through continuous biometric monitoring, the AI construct is enabled to discover overarching patterns that may reveal the underlying reason for poorly controlled sugar. For example, a nightly elevated glucose may be the result of dinner preferences rich in carbohydrates. This type of solution effectively increases affordability of healthcare (through reduction of ER visits), improves access to useful healthcare information, reduces the potential for human error, and generally improves health outcomes.

The following other potential uses for AI within healthcare also have been explored:

1. Making sense of complex and contradictory healthcare data
2. Integration of sensor-collected biometric data into diagnostic alerts
3. Compliance with medications and other time-sensitive treatments
4. Wellness and health behavior strategies
5. Enforcement of Standards of Care Guidelines when using ancillary providers
6. Physical robots to deliver healthcare needs or medications

# PART VI

## SARS-COV-2 PANDEMIC LESSONS FOR OUR HEALTHCARE

CHAPTER 1

# SARS-COV-2 PANDEMIC LESSONS FOR OUR HEALTHCARE

No review of the healthcare system will be complete without an analysis of the largest healthcare crisis of the past century, the SARS-CoV-2 pandemic, which began in December 2019 and still impacts our lives at present.

It is important to recognize the heroic efforts of medical workers during this COVID-19 pandemic. They have been rightfully praised and honored as heroes for their work in saving hundreds of thousands of lives during one of the most horrific periods in medical history. From a systems perspective, the COVID-19 pandemic has revealed invaluable lessons about our healthcare system and, importantly, where the deficiencies are.

## A Worldwide Pandemic Can Still Threaten Our Lives and Livelihoods

In December 2019, a report from the Chinese city of Wuhan indicated the emergence of a new virus that may have originated from animals, possibly bats, before spreading to humans.[88] Infections resulted in significant respiratory dysfunction that contributed to its high mortality rate. In early January 2020, the virus was identified as SARS-CoV-2, or COVID-19, with the appended number representing the year in which the virus was discovered. Within a few months, the deadly virus spread across the world, causing the worst global health crisis in the past 100 years.

During the pandemic, the world faced unprecedented challenges, affecting nearly every aspect of life. The virus quickly spread across the globe and many health systems proved ill-equipped to handle the stress. The United States struggled to provide adequate preventive and therapeutic responses to the pandemic. At the time of this writing (May 2022), the United States had almost 84 million cases of COVID-19 infection, and one million Americans had died from the virus.[88]

Within every domain of life, from physical and mental health to financial stability, our society felt the heavy burden that the pandemic imposed onto our lives. The global economy plummeted as jobs evaporated. In 2020, the global gross domestic product declined by 6.7% as a result of the COVID-19 pandemic.[89] Working Americans felt the financial impact of this pandemic, as the unemployment rate skyrocketed from 3.7% in 2019 to 8.1% in 2020.

One of the most astonishing impacts of the COVID-19 pandemic was the now apparent defects of our healthcare system. Giving credit where credit is due, I admit that the state of biomedical technology allowed the world's scientific community to create vaccines—from identifying the virus' RNA sequence, to the creation of RNA-based vaccines, to FDA emergency use authorization—at "warp speed" compared to historical vaccine development initiatives.[88] On the other hand, the virus so clearly demonstrated our healthcare system's inability to prevent, mitigate, and eliminate chronic conditions that, in the presence of SARS-CoV-2, led to hundreds of thousands of deaths among Americans.

## Chronic Conditions Are the Real Causes of Death in any Healthcare Crisis

Chronic conditions, by definition, are diseases that an affected individual carries for a long period of time before ultimately becoming fatal due to downstream complications. However, these conditions become immediate causes of mortality when an affected person falls ill with a virus like SARS-CoV-2. Those with preexisting chronic conditions like obesity, diabetes, and cardiovascular diseases are far more likely to require a ventilator for support or die from a COVID-19 infection. Among the one million dead Americans, a majority featured individuals that, as a result of their preexisting chronic conditions, developed severe, complicated infections that ultimately required ventilators or other dangerous medical interventions in an attempt to prolong their lives.

In any healthcare crisis, we can understand that chronic conditions are the leading risk factors for fatality. Those who suffer from obesity, diabetes, cardiovascular diseases, or other chronic medical issues exhibit more fragile health states, which feature weakened immune systems and less resilience for staying healthy. For example, people who have type 1 or 2 diabetes and fall ill with COVID-19 are faced with an increased risk of complications like diabetic ketoacidosis, which can lead to sepsis and septic shock.[91] As another example, obesity is associated with impaired immunity and can make ventilation more difficult and decrease lung capacity. According to the CDC, more than 900,000 adult COVID-19 hospitalizations have occurred in the United States from the start of the pandemic until November of 2020. Among this number, models estimate that 271,800, or 30.2%, of these hospitalizations were attributed to obesity alone.[92]

Data from nearly 150,000 U.S. adults diagnosed with COVID-19 from March to December 2020 showed that half of these adults were obese and around an additional 28% were overweight, based on their body mass index (BMI). Among individuals infected with COVID-19, the risk of hospitalization, admission to the intensive care unit, and death rates were the lowest among patients whose BMI was in or around the healthy range of 18.5–24.9; consequently, the risk of complicated infections rose sharply as BMI increased. For patients with a BMI between 30 and 34.9, it was observed that these individuals had a 7% increased risk of hospitalization, an 8% increased risk of dying, and a 35% increased risk of requiring mechanical ventilation when compared with patients of a healthy weight. The risk of requiring mechanical ventilation among individuals with the highest BMIs (>45) was double that of patients with a healthy weight. Additionally, patients with the highest BMIs were linked to a 61% increased risk of death and a 33% increased risk of hospitalization compared to those with a healthy weight. The authors of this report concluded that "the findings in this report highlight a dose-response relationship between higher BMI and severe COVID-19 associated illness and underscore the need for more progressively intensive illness management as obesity severity increases."[93]

## Public Health Departments Are Insufficient in Protecting Our Personal Health

The heartbreaking number of people who have died from COVID-19 demonstrates that our public health departments profoundly lack the ability to protect the health of our population. Certainly part of this inability stems from a lack of proper funds to make an impact within communities. According to *Kaiser Health News* and the *Associated Press*, "since 2010, spending for state public health departments has dropped by 18% per capita and spending for local health departments has fallen by 16%."[94] Due to this steady decrease in funding, public health departments were ill-equipped to deal with the demands of the pandemic. "Public health is in disarray" was the conclusion of a study conducted by the National Academy of Medicine that was published in 1988 titled, "The Future of Public Health in the United States."[95] Decades later, the COVID-19 pandemic revealed this disarray in full view.

Over the past few decades, a lack of funding and budgetary priority for public health departments, both at the state and local levels, has caused a steady decline in the quality of public health services. Employment within public health departments has decreased since the 2008 recession, and no significant effort has been made to reverse this trend or improve the quality of services. This trend continues at present, as public health departments have not been able to stage a significant response to the COVID-19 pandemic beyond handwashing tutorials and vaccine encouragement. <u>Our population, wrought with chronic conditions that neither handwashing nor vaccines can eradicate, desperately needs a public health intervention that far surpasses this superficial level of help.</u>

Budgetary constraints aside, our public health system has not been able to adapt to the foremost health threat to our population, which is the escalating prevalence of chronic medical conditions. We need a system that can prioritize the prevention, mitigation, and elimination of chronic medical conditions; the pandemic has taught us that these diseases are not only the most dangerous but also the most persistent threats to living healthy, productive, and fulfilling lives.

## Hospital-Based Delivery System Is in the Sole Business of Sick Care

The COVID-19 pandemic also demonstrated that hospitals are almost exclusively sites of sick care, as that is how their business models are designed to operate and grow. With its focus planted on delivering sick care services, our sick care system met a profound shortage in capacity when so many people fell severely ill during the pandemic. Hospitals, the core of our healthcare delivery system, eventually had capacity only for the sickest of the sick. They were, therefore, unable to provide care for members of the community who were exposed to COVID-19, who looked to this system for testing, information, and many other healthcare needs of those who had not become infected with COVID-19. Non-ill individuals accounted for 80%–90% of the population during the COVID-19 pandemic, therefore, the vast majority of the population required non-sick care services that our hospital-based sick care system could not offer during this time.

From a systems perspective, it became clear that for all the resources that we funnel into our hospital-based sick care system, its operational capacity could not be used for any purpose other than to take care of the sickest of the sick. As a result, many large corporations, community centers, and other institutions that had turned to the hospital system for help were left with the sour conclusion that hospitals were not designed to keep people healthy, but rather to deliver sick care.

## There Is a Gap between the Public Health and Hospital-Based Sick Care System

The COVID-19 pandemic taught me one major lesson: there is a systemic gap in our healthcare system between the services provided by public health and the hospital-based sick care system. My initial observation took place during early 2020, when our nation was locked down and it was clear that public health departments were inadequately resourced to deal with the massive demand for testing, tracking, and many other needs that the COVID-19 pandemic had created. At the same time, hospitals were so overwhelmed treating patients suffering from COVID-19 in concert with preexisting chronic conditions, they were unable to respond to health care needs of the majority of the population (80%–90%) who were not sick enough to require hospital inpatient care and were generally following public health directives by wearing masks, staying at home, and social distancing. For this majority, our healthcare system, with around 5,000 hospitals nationwide, provided no benefit at all. This massive and expensive healthcare system could not help the lion's share of our population with their routine health needs. Those individuals experiencing issues related or unrelated to COVID-19 with common, non-threatening symptoms like headaches and sore throats, or other individuals with diabetes, arthritis, or many other medical issues, could not be helped by our sick care system. Instead, Dr. Google or anecdotal advice from friends and family were the only resources these individuals could access for their needs.

Later, I discovered that the explanation for this systemic gap is simple and clear. As we have discussed earlier, we have built the existing segments of our healthcare system (public health and a hospital-based sick care system) with the priority of eradicating infectious diseases in the early 20th century—then allocating resources to developing diagnostic and therapeutic solutions for the next set of killers such as cardiovascular disease, cancer, traumatic injuries, and common complications of chronic conditions. By their nature, the diagnostic and therapeutic solutions only come into play AFTER symptoms of diseases have appeared or are detected by screening tools such as pap smear, mammographies, and colonoscopies. In this system, no doctor will see you if you don't have a "chief complaint." However, after more than a century of research into the pathophysiology of major causes of death, we now know that the initial damaging changes in our bodies (at the molecular, cellular, or organ levels) happen years before any symptoms or chief complaints appear. It is during this time period where the risk factors (such as high cholesterol, inflammation, oxidative stress, physiologic stress, and mental stress) work their way through the immune systems and natural defense mechanisms of our bodies. If they succeed in overwhelming our immunity and defense systems, then we become ill and succumb to those diseases and their complications. So in a complete model, we must pay attention to those health risk factors and ideally get help from a group of professionals equipped with knowledge and tools to help us to eliminate or reduce the impact of these risk factors. If we can collectively do that job correctly, we could reduce the chance of getting sick and not needing the sick care services for those conditions. An analogy could be drawn with the COVID-19 pandemic. If we could reduce the risk of exposure to COVID-19, and get a vaccination, we could avoid getting the COVID-19 disease altogether.

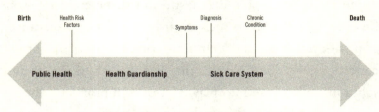

The gap in healthcare according to natural history of disease development

During those early months of the COVID-19 pandemic, the question on my mind was: At the system level, who or which segment of healthcare should take care of us when we are not sick and are continuously facing health risk factors in our lives? Should such a system exist? If yes, who should build it or be in charge of it? Who should pay for it? My thoughts sparked a chain of questions that followed the initial impression that our nation needs a sector in between public health and hospital-based sick care systems.

The stark answer was that no segment currently exists to fulfill this purpose. The revealing lesson of COVID-19 for me was that there is a gaping hole in between the two segments of our healthcare. This gap could be filled by a new segment that I like to call the "Health Guardianship": an independent segment whose focus, practice, and business model would be to keep the population and individuals healthy. The establishment of this new segment parallels the realization we had at the beginning of the 20th century that individuals cannot be left to their own resources to deal with infectious disease (water and food sanitation, vaccination programs, and outbreak control.) This past realization led to the creation of the public health segment of our healthcare system. The rising rates of chronic conditions that consume our healthcare resources and healthy years of our lives parallels the early years of the 20th century.

**Lifelong Health Needs**

| Public Health | Health Guardians<br>Reduce Chronic Conditions<br>Protect Health | Hospital Based Sick Care |

COVID-19

# PART VII
# HOW TO FIX THE SYSTEM AND NOT BANDAGE IT?

When there are systematic errors within any system, the system necessarily creates "bad" results, or results that are incompatible with the system's intentions. These systematic errors are different in nature from the occasional random error that may happen in even the best system or organization. I propose that the previously described misalignments represent systematic errors in the U.S. healthcare system that must be recognized and fixed. If they are not fixed, we may expect the same dismal results in the future: massive waste and poor outcomes. Here we will review various opportunities for fixing the systematic errors in our healthcare system.

CHAPTER 1

# REDUCE THE WASTE BY FIXING THE MISALIGNMENTS

The first step toward fixing our healthcare system must be the realignment of the role of doctors, especially those that serve as PCPs who keep consumers healthy. A landmark study published in the New England Journal of Medicine indicates that >90% of the Western populations' healthcare needs fall within the domain of primary care. [135] Less than 5% of healthcare needs are related to sick care services offered by hospitals and specialists.[96] However, distribution of spending is almost a complete reversal of these needs, where >90% of healthcare spending is paid for the non-primary care services, as those specialty care services are expensive and the main driver of the hospitals' revenues.

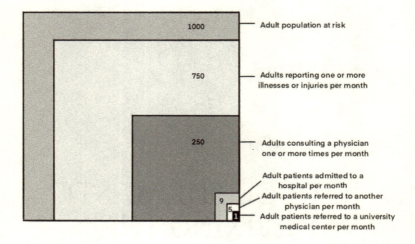

The realignment between PCPs and consumers must be reorganized and fixed. Rather than financially incentivizing PCPs to contribute to the current financial goals of hospitals by acting as referral machines, PCPs should instead be incentivized to identify and mitigate health risks of the individuals under their care. And their interventions should happen long before an individual's impending health risks manifest as illnesses to be treated through sick care.

In the current system, the jobs of PCPs are to diagnose and treat medical conditions after a chief complaint has developed. At present, medical students are not taught to fill a role in identifying individuals who may develop a chief complaint in the future. When a medical student becomes a physician, they sit in an office, and individuals currently experiencing symptoms receive their attention, again only after these symptoms develop. For example, if I do not already have hypertension, I cannot go to my doctor seeking impactful advice. Can you imagine making an appointment, arriving at the office of a physician who is busy with patients experiencing all sorts of complex ailments, and asking her, "Could you please help me not develop hypertension, chest pain, or a lump in my breast during the next 30 years of my life?" The most likely outcome is that she would look at you in confusion and refer you to Dr. Google to find your answers! Or, at best, she would give you some superficial and generic advice on how to eat healthy and exercise. However, as soon as you have a symptom report, or the physician diagnoses a disease, she will present to you a whole list of detailed (and often expensive) options for further evaluation and treatment. When it comes to helping you to not develop symptoms, her solution is as good as yours: Dr. Google!

PCPs becoming the agent of the consumer would allow them to use their clinical skills toward providing primary care, coordination of care, and communication with others such as mental health providers and nutritionists who could be pulled together to provide "person centered" care to the consumer. The first step in disrupting the system from a sick care toward a "health care" begins with realignment of the role of PCPs.

CHAPTER 2

# REWARD GUARDIANSHIP OF HEALTH, NOT DELIVERY OF SICK CARE SERVICES

The next fix must create business models in which guardianship of health by the providers, especially PCPs, and not delivery of sick care services, is rewarded. To put this situation in the context of current medical knowledge, at present, we have a large body of scientific data on the role of risk factors for diseases and how to identify them before symptoms develop. Upon recognition, those risk factors can be mitigated to minimize the possibility that symptoms and their conditions would appear in the future. Given this corpus of biomedical knowledge, the PCPs would be engaged in the delivery of services aimed at mitigating health risk factors, which would amount to keeping people healthy. These services are not consistent with the business models and financial goals of the current hospital-based sick care system. Therefore, they remain underdeveloped, and providers do not offer or even acknowledge these services. We will discuss the science and art of health risk mitigation in the next part of this book to demonstrate how similar approaches in other industries have led to elimination of disease-like hazards in those industries.

Academics and payers have recently recognized that this misalignment must be fixed both at the clinical and business levels. Both employer-funded payers in the private sector and CMS in the public sector have recognized the key role that PCPs must fill in guarding the health of an individual. As a result, over the past two decades, government-backed initiatives have pushed for the creation of healthcare delivery models in which PCPs are responsible for the overall health of their patients and are rewarded for keeping individuals healthy. Among these models is the DPC model, in which the consumer subscribes to a PCP's care via a monthly fee. CMS and other payers have created similar models, including "Value-Based Programs," which reward PCPs for lowering the cost of sick care among their patient panel. We will explore this concept further in a later chapter.

CHAPTER 3

# FREE TO CHOOSE! CONSUMERS MUST BE IN CONTROL OF THEIR MONEY!

The next fix relates to the control of payments for healthcare services that must shift to the consumer and away from the third-party payers. Significant scientific and market-based data indicates that, for more than 95% of the needs of a population, the healthcare services that would fulfill them are "shoppable," which means that patients may "shop" for services and providers to find better providers at a cheaper price. In a true life-or-death emergency, a person does not have the time or serenity to make this type of decision for herself; but true emergencies constitute less than 3% of all situations that require healthcare. Somehow in the medical field, the consumer (you and I, the individual) has been rendered incompetent in making decisions on which provider should deliver healthcare and how much should be spent on it. Within the current payment system, the authority of decisions on healthcare spending for the majority of American adults is relinquished to employers, who in collaboration with insurance companies and multiple layers of intermediaries make the decisions for what services we can use and how much they should be paid for. Similarly, the federal government, via CMS, controls the payment for selection of medical services for another 100 million Americans.

Individuals only see their out-of-pocket fees, and this gives rise to the illusion that individuals only pay for this small portion of the total healthcare expense. But in reality, it is the individual that foots the less-visible expenses paid from employers and the federal government to insurance companies and providers. It is estimated that an American worker contributes a total of $1.2 million from the age of 26 to the age of 65 toward premiums and other healthcare expenses.[137] This $1.2 million is gradually deducted from lost earnings of workers and Medicare contributions in tax payments throughout the working years. **Therefore, workers and taxpayers are the true ultimate payers for the nation's healthcare expense; therefore, they should have a say on how it is spent.**

From an ethical perspective, an individual must have the ultimate responsibility and authority in making decisions about her own health. Individuals must have total visibility over healthcare expenditure information and control over their healthcare funds. To accomplish this, an individual must be able to use the funds allocated to that individual's health (which may come from an employer or CMS) to directly pay for services that she believes providers are offering to improve her health.

Implementing this change in the control of money will lead to efficiency in the healthcare system, as it would reinstitute free market principles in an environment where they are not currently present. The free market has created the most efficient models in all industries in which it is allowed to exist. It does this by optimizing the lowest price for the highest quality based on the supply of providers and demand of consumers, and in some cases, functions with little government control. With nearly two centuries of experience in free markets, many industries in our nation have demonstrated the free market's efficacy in reducing waste, controlling cost, and improving quality for the benefit of the payer, who is usually the consumer. The reinstitution of free market forces is exactly what the healthcare industry needs. A consumer who sees and controls the spending of her money is in the best position to reduce waste.

The question remains: how can this restructuring be achieved when third-party payers have existed in the healthcare system for almost a century?

The answer brings good news. A similar transformation took place in another part of our lives during the last part of the 20th century. During the 1970s, systematic errors in how pension plans were funded and controlled led to the passing of the Employees Retirement and Safety Act of 1974.[123] Under this law, and its subsequent iterations, the control and decision-making for pensions and retirement savings were transferred from employers to employees as individuals. As a result, individual retirement accounts (IRAs) and their variations proliferated. Following that transformation, many financial institutions (such as Fidelity, Vanguard, and Charles Schwab) became the agents of the employees' retirement funds. In essence, they became "guardians" for retirement security of employees, using funds that were provided by their employers. A small set of additional regulatory changes today may give rise to a similar transformation in healthcare funding.

A recent advancement, individual coverage health reimbursement accounts (ICHRAs), may form the cornerstone of such a transformation. This concept was initiated by President Trump but has since received endorsement from the Biden administration. Under the regulations of ICHRAs, employers may transfer designated funds for health insurance premiums or other medical expenses to their employees. These funds will be tax free to employees and are tax-exempt expenses for the employers; this is very similar to regulations surrounding traditional health insurance plans, called "defined benefits."

Unlike defined benefits plans, the approach of ICHRAs (called "defined contribution" plans) give employers significant budget control, but provides the ultimate decision making of healthcare payments to employees. This follows a very similar pattern to IRAs for retirement funds. By restructuring authority in making decisions for healthcare purchases, the employee/individual will gain transparency toward the total cost of care. And, like all other areas that obey free market principles, by giving control of funds to the ultimate payer/consumer, costs are lowered, outcomes are improved, and efficiency is maximized.

CHAPTER 4

# DISRUPT THE SYSTEM TOWARD HEALTHCARE AND AWAY FROM SICK CARE!

The existence of the gap between the two segments of healthcare to address the needs of people when they are not sick, and misalignments in the hospital-based sick care system, would make the job of fixing the system impossible without a true disruption. This is analogous to the case of an old building where the cost and energy needed to fix all its problems is much more than erasing it and building a new one. I am not recommending erasing the existing segments of the healthcare system, but instead recommending adopting a disruptive mindset when thinking about fixing the healthcare system. A disruptive mindset would start by seeing the contrast between a sick care versus a healthcare system by recognizing that the existing Sick Care System delivers:

a. Reactive care
b. Interventions <u>after</u> symptoms have appeared
c. Episodic and fragmented care
d. Provider-centric scheduling practices
e. Fee-for-service reimbursement models
f. Solutions that rely on expertise of one

Whereas a **Healthcare System** should deliver:

a. Proactive care
b. Focusing on reduction of risk factors way before appearance of symptoms or diseases
c. Continuous and coordinated care and wellness
d. Personal, consumer centric model in its delivery
e. Solutions that rely on knowledge and expertise of many in the age of democratization of health information
f. Rewards for desired outcomes

In order to deliver such a healthcare model, the disruptive mindset would subsequently ask:

1. How can above-mentioned elements of a healthcare system be delivered in an integrated manner that would result in easy access, affordable, and high-quality services to everyone?

2. How can it realign the relationship between the providers and the consumers of services so the doctor's job would be to keep people healthy and out of the hospitals rather than benefiting from people being sick and filling the hospitals?
3. How can advances in technology lead to lower cost of services similar to any other industry?
4. How can disciplines of a free market supply and demand relationship be applied where the consumer—the ultimate payer—has control over her choices and spending?

Further, a disruptive model will require innovation and must not include cookie-cutter solutions such as a single-payer model or Medicare-for-all. A disruptive model for U.S. healthcare must be born out of innovative solutions conceived and tested within this nation's healthcare system. Nearly 70 years of expansions in government-sponsored single-payer programs affecting nearly 100 million Americans have not been able to make a dent in the cost of sick care or lower the prevalence of chronic conditions; nor have they been able to heal the financial misalignments present within the system or even properly describe them. We must redesign this wasteful healthcare engine and realign its functional components; and only then may American healthcare lead the world in ushering in a 21st-century healthcare system where *everyone* has access to affordable, high tech, and high quality healthcare services regardless of who they are and where they live.

# PART VIII
# HEALTH GUARDIANSHIP: THE NEW AND MISSING PIECE FOR A POST-PANDEMIC HEALTHCARE SYSTEM

CHAPTER 1

# FILL THE EXISTING GAP BETWEEN PUBLIC HEALTH AND THE HOSPITAL-BASED SICK CARE SYSTEM

We have reviewed the health score of our nation to demonstrate the escalation of chronic conditions and prevalence of medical errors, two of the major contributors to America's leading causes of death during the first two decades of the 21st century. This simple and yet potent observation indicates that there is a deep flaw, a chasm between the health needs of our people and the services currently provided by the existing system. We believe this also indicates the need for a third and independent segment that can fill the gap between what public health departments and what the hospital-based sick care systems provide. We propose that we need to create and establish a new segment whose sole mission is to mitigate health risks at the personal level and to develop strategies to prevent chronic conditions at the public level. Establishment of a new segment will allow us to focus and integrate services at various levels of healthcare, including the individual, family, community, and public levels; thus, further exploring the need for mitigation of health risks that cause chronic medical conditions and their associated morbidity and mortality.

The goal of this newly established segment will be to combine the knowledge and insight we have acquired over the past century in population health science, clinical medicine, genetics, environmental health, and any other scientific areas that would allow us to help individuals better protect their health. All relevant science and technology must be integrated <u>toward creating a personalized health risk mitigation system to prevent and eliminate chronic conditions</u>, just as we did to smallpox and other leading causes of death in the past century.

For its business model, the new segment would likely function as a subscription and at-risk model. The payment for this segment would be a part of healthcare payment sponsored by employers or the federal government, just as sick care is.

This new segment or organization would fill the existing gap between our public health departments and the hospital-based sick care system. The need for this new segment was made apparent during the COVID-19 pandemic. Now, we understand that 80%–90% of our society has an unmet need for advice and assistance in daily life toward achieving and sustaining health. The new segment would directly address chronic condition risk factors such as obesity, diabetes, cardiovascular diseases, musculoskeletal illness, and other chronic conditions that the CDC has deemed almost entirely preventable. Ultimately, we will work toward reducing the probability of premature death, such as those we saw during the COVID-19 pandemic.

This new segment of the health care system holds as its fundamental value the goal of keeping people healthy. We can call this new segment "Health Guardianship." This segment can be built from existing primary care practices, which will function as the core of Health Guardians.

CHAPTER 2

# CHRONIC CONDITIONS MUST GO! THE MOONSHOT IS POSSIBLE

It is clear that the major results of the 20th century for our healthcare system have been: 1) the escalation of chronic conditions among Americans; and 2) a hospital-based delivery system whose business model significantly benefits from this escalation, regardless of what they say in their marketing campaigns. Six out of ten Americans have at least one chronic condition, and four out of ten have two or more[59] chronic conditions such as hypertension, coronary artery disease, obesity, diabetes, and mental health disorders. These conditions contribute to the leading causes of death among Americans. For example, more than 868,000 Americans die of heart disease or stroke every year—one-third of all deaths in the United States.[97]

The increasing prevalence of chronic conditions creates significant problems for the health of our nation during the 21st century. As exemplified by the healthcare cost of obesity, chronic conditions are the cause of ballooning health expenses. In 2016 the total cost in the United States for direct healthcare treatment for chronic health conditions totaled $1.1 trillion— nearly 6% of the nation's GDP. The most expensive of these conditions, in terms of direct healthcare costs, is: (1) diabetes, which is estimated to exceed $300 billion; (2) mental health and Alzheimer's disease, which exceeds $500 billion; and (3) osteoarthritis and musculoskeletal conditions, which is estimated to cost about $300 billion. Ninety percent of the nation's spending is for people with chronic conditions.[98]

Chronic conditions are also a source of unnecessary care in our hospital-based system. People with chronic conditions use over 75% of hospital days, outpatient office visits, home healthcare services, and prescription drugs in the United States. They are also more likely to suffer from medical errors and harms that are associated with hospitalization and other unnecessary diagnostic and therapeutic services.

The most fascinating part of our examination of chronic conditions in America is that nearly all of them are related to choices made in our daily lives and, as scientific evidence indicates, are entirely preventable. The CDC acknowledges that most, if not all, of these chronic conditions are caused by a shortlist of risk behaviors, including tobacco use[99] and exposure to secondhand smoke, poor nutrition[100] (including diets low in fruits and vegetables and high in sodium and saturated fats), lack of physical activity,[101] and excessive alcohol use.[102]

Actress Angelina Jolie opted to have a double mastectomy as a risk mitigation for prevention of development of breast cancer when she discovered that she has the genetic mutation for developing the disease.[104] But, not all risk mitigations need to be as radical as this instance. For example, the diagram below[105] shows us a figure from a review article published in *Lancet Neurology*, discussing the risk factors related to Alzheimer's disease. The risk factors contributing to the development of Alzheimer's start from the young age of 20.

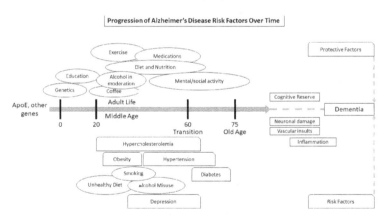

This review shows that many aspects of our lives starting as early as in our 20s, like physical activity, alcohol consumption, and nutrition, greatly impact our chance of developing diseases like Alzheimer's disease and these are all factors within our control. We propose that with technological advances directed toward this purpose, health risk mitigation can be explored even at the tissue, cellular, and molecular level, so specific targeting of those risks in addition to lifestyle modifications could be implemented with the goal of elimination or dramatic reduction of risk of diseases such as Alzheimer's, obesity, and diabetes. As depicted below, proactive identification and mitigation of many health risk factors related to chronic conditions will give us the best chance to change the direction of disease development and intensity of its presence in our lives. All these factors are present long before developing any symptoms that would be detected by screening or other diagnostic tools currently used in the sick care system.

### Natural History of Any Disease

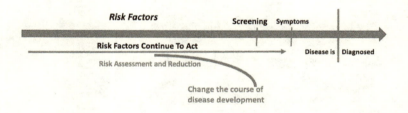

Similar scientific data is available for almost all other chronic conditions that have affected our nation during the 20th and 21st centuries. Evidence suggests that the majority, if not all, of these chronic conditions are preventable if these risk factors are mitigated at both individual and societal levels. This concept and course of action is similar to how infectious diseases were eradicated from our society by a combination of individual awareness of the risk of infections and public health efforts.

Washing hands before meals, providing clean water sources, the refrigeration of food, inspections of restaurants, colony count of lakes, and the vaccination of children collectively led to the elimination of infectious diseases as the number one cause of death in the previous century. We must take a similar approach toward eliminating chronic conditions as the most common roots of causes of death and deterioration of quality of life.

CHAPTER 3

# HEALTH RISK MANAGEMENT INSTEAD OF DISEASE MANAGEMENT

During the same period that we have advanced in diagnostic and treatment knowledge and technologies to take care of our diseases, we have also made advancements in the science behind risk management in various industries such as air travel, fire prevention, car safety, and other industries where we have tremendously reduced hazards that threaten lives. As a result, we learned how to identify categories of risks and continuously eliminate the risk of hazardous events such as airline crashes, fires, chemical spills, and car accidents.

As an example, air travel has become the safest mode of transportation. This is due to the industry's effective use of risk management strategies. Since the Wright Brothers[122] made their first flight, we have advanced our knowledge, skills, and airline services to make airplanes the safest mode of transportation. It is currently safer to fly in an airplane than travel any distance on the ground via vehicles or animals.[104] Such safety was created by establishing a system that continuously monitors machines and processes through well-defined checklists, from preflight to initial take off, to cruising, and to landing. This allows for an amazing, seamless integration of more than a thousand operations that function simultaneously to bring safe and affordable flight and air transportation to everyone.

When comparing the 5,000-year history of medicine to the mere 117 years that the airline industry has operated, it is appalling that we have not successfully stopped or stalled the creation of health hazards such as diabetes, obesity, or cardiovascular problems. We have actually done the opposite of risk prevention; we've added medical errors to the list of leading causes of death in the United States.

We can also look to fire risk management for success stories in mitigating risks and prevention of fires instead of dealing with burned buildings or bodies. Fires are commonly understood as a threat that has risked the lives of people for centuries. But, throughout history, we have used science and problem solving to prevent harm and death from it. Our lifestyles in the United States, and most of the western world, feature a series of personal, household, work, and societal mitigation strategies that function in harmony to prevent the overall risk of fires in our households or workplaces. For example, in our personal lives, we train children how to be cognizant of fire risks, how to safely escape buildings, and a handful of other fire prevention drills. In our households we follow certain fire hazard rules such as installing and maintaining fire detectors and having fire extinguishers readily available. Likewise, our workplaces function under strict fire prevention measures. Lastly, at the societal level, we have separated fire risk mitigation into local, state, and governmental levels. We have placed fire departments in every community where they serve to protect and educate. We use trained personnel of fire departments to extinguish fires when they occur, and we honor them as local heroes who teach our children to save lives.

Once more, the long history and development of fire safety parallels the extensive history we have with medical developments and the healthcare system. We have several thousand years of knowledge of risks to our health and at least 100 years of intimate knowledge and scientific insight into risk factors for diabetes, obesity, cardiovascular diseases, Alzheimer's disease, and many other chronic medical conditions at the cellular, tissue, and organ levels. We have access to some of the most sophisticated technological tools to detect, change, and alter those risk factors; and yet, our health risk mitigation policies still seem small compared to our successes in areas like fires and airline travel. Why have we not felt motivated nor had the infrastructure to systematically reduce the risk of developing chronic conditions? The answer is simple. We have not had an organization or segment in our healthcare system whose business model profits from keeping people healthy. It is time for us to create a new segment of healthcare and to define its business model.

CHAPTER 4

# A BOW-TIE RISK MANAGEMENT SEGMENT FOR HEALTHCARE

The bow-tie model, or figure, has been used in many industries and is a common model for understanding and improving risk management.

If we imagine the shape of a bow tie (see below), the left side of the knot facing us conveys the causes of an event in the forms of both threat and opportunity. By balancing those two aspects, we can cultivate strategies for decreasing or increasing the likelihood of that event.

On the right side of the knot, we weigh the consequences of the event to allow us to minimize loss. As we can understand, the bow-tie model ultimately captures the whole timeline of a risky event in a single snapshot.

In order to appropriately address and manage health risks, we must design the new segment of our healthcare system to minimize loss through several functions. If we return to our fire example, from left to right, our various fire risk prevention systems work towards a singular goal. Firefighters who help reduce loss during and after the event are also involved with training individuals and educating children on how to prevent fires and rescue themselves in the event of a fire. Even though there is a bifurcation in fire risk mitigation strategies between what individuals or firefighters and fire departments do, we are able to align the functions to work toward a common goal, namely to help prevent the loss associated with fire and promote a person's well-being.

The bow-tie model shows both the successful and unsuccessful models of risk mitigation. In the case of airlines and fire risk mitigation, we have put significant effort to the left side of the bow tie to identify and optimize the prevention methodologies to prevent an airline crash or a fire from happening. At the same time, we have established state and federal agencies who oversee the efforts of the whole system. When a hazardous event happens (airline crash or a fire), these agencies gather information, analyze the data, and gain more insight about the incident. They identify what went wrong and how we can do a better job in risk mitigation going forward. Now, after about 100 years of flying, the chances of an airline crash are statistically impossible to predict.

With the same systems, we have protected major skyscrapers such as the Empire State Building and Sears Tower and many others around the country from hazards of fire for more than half a century. However, in the model of healthcare, the hospital-based sick care system is entirely focused on the right side of the bow tie, and primarily focuses on either exploiting needs after a disease has happened or providing recovery resources after the health injury or disease has occurred. At the same time, public health departments have moved away from providing services to prevent chronic conditions, as they lack the resources and infrastructure to be able to help us at the personal level. We should acknowledge that public health departments do a great job in preventing infectious diseases by instituting mandates aimed at reducing the risk of communicable diseases to our societies. However, <u>we need a new segment that focuses on identifying and optimizing risks related to chronic conditions such as obesity, diabetes, and cardiovascular diseases</u>.

This new segment—Health Guardianship—must use a combination of clinical knowledge, genetics, population health, socioeconomic status, risk management, personal behavior, decision-making process, and many other branches of science that have developed over the past century to guard the consumer's health.

Scientific data that has been vigorously generated over the past 100 years clearly demonstrates that the majority of chronic medical conditions are the results of lifestyle choices and are therefore modifiable. We only need a business model for organizations to put this knowledge to productive work. Like the many advances we have made in other industries in the past century, this segment will distill and apply relevant scientific discoveries and provide accountability for protecting the health of populations. This new segment would ultimately lead to those promised results that the current hospital-based sick care system has consistently failed to deliver: a population healthy enough to live vigorously to the ninth and tenth decades of their lives without suffering from chronic medical conditions.

CHAPTER 5

# HOW WOULD THE NEW SEGMENT OF HEALTH GUARDIANSHIP WORK?

In this chapter, we will explain some of the underlying disciplines and frameworks on which Health Guardianship can be formed and operated on.

## Mission

The mission of Health Guardianship is to use all the available scientific, clinical, behavioral economics, and other discoveries to protect and improve the health of a person. Health data indicates that no person is 100% sick or 100% healthy. A 100% sick person does not live among us any longer, and a 100% healthy person has not been born yet! One's state of health is the result of a balance between the forces of health and illness within our body that are the results of nature (genetics) and nurture (lifestyle) factors. A prime example is that we live among billions of germs in our environment, but only become affected by them (getting sick or infected) when either our immune system becomes weak (our health forces are reduced) or the growth of germs overwhelms our forces of health (like COVID-19). The more we can strengthen our forces of health (proper nutrition, physical activity, rest, etc.), the more likely we are to remain healthy. The more exposure we have to sources of illness (such as exposure to germs and bacteria, excessive calories, and little physical activity), the more likely sources of illness will weigh the balance towards either making us ill or promoting chronic conditions such as obesity, diabetes, and arthritis. The mission of Health Guardianship is to help us to strengthen our forces of health.

## Business Principles

The following principles must apply to the Health Guardianship business structure:

1. *The buyer's agent*: Health Guardians must be financially aligned with the consumer and profit in proportion to the quality of health outcomes that the consumer experiences. As in any other buyer's agency, the provider of the service would be financially incentivized to provide clearly defined or mutually agreed-upon outcomes. A financial alignment between the Health Guardians and the consumer is the

cornerstone of a healthy business relationship that works for both parties.

2. *Control by the consumer*: The consumer must be in control of the payment for healthcare expenses. Similar to any other industry in a free market-based society, the consumer of a good must be the ultimate decision maker on what services and providers they use and what price is paid. Because of the complexity of medicine, the consumer may use the advice of a Health Guardian to determine what services are needed and a fair market price. This relationship would be like that of financial advisors, who advise the investor/consumer about technical details of an investment. Health Guardians could provide technical medical information to the consumer without being the ultimate decision maker. All decision-making authority would remain with the consumer.

## Delivery Model

According to the above principles, the consumer would direct and participate in the management of her health and the overall utilization of healthcare. With the consumer at the "driver's seat of the bus," the Health Guardians would function as the passengers of that bus, channeling expert knowledge to provide technical information to the driver. The following clinical and scientific models could be applied to delivery and operations of Health Guardianship:

A. *Customized, person-centered essential care planning*: Health Guardianships will integrate the disciplines of primary care, preventive care, behavioral health, nutrition, fitness, and biometric monitoring to create customized, person-centered care and health improvement plans. Those plans would be maintained on an ongoing basis, and its details would be shared transparently between health guardians and the consumer as a road map toward health improvement. We call this level of health services "Essential Care." The road map for "customized, person-centered, essential care" (CPCEC) will have assigned tasks and desired goals for each party involved in guarding the consumer's health. Involved parties may include consumers, PCPs, behavioral therapists, nutritionists, fitness coaches, nurses, and other advisors. Tools that can aid in continuous monitoring of health risks in a person and provide guidance and corrective actions to avoid health hazards, illnesses, or chronic conditions can be integrated into this model. In a similar manner to how risks are handled in the airline industry, a set of checklists could be applied to every aspect of a person's health; receiving longitudinal data from wearable or non-wearable sensors that would allow ongoing monitoring, and warnings, or other tools that would help to mitigate health risks to a person. We may note that, in the airline industry, it is too late to prevent an air crash after the engine is on fire at an altitude of 30,000 feet! Preventing crashes starts from the preflight stage and continues throughout the life of a flight by receiving continuous data from thousands of sensors that are embedded throughout the body of the airplane. As another successful example, hundreds of sensors are also embedded in our modern cars, which provides proactive alerts for impending issues and dramatically reduces downstream breakdowns. Similarly, the risks for chronic conditions such as obesity, diabetes, Alzheimer's, and other conditions don't start when the first symptoms have appeared, they start as early as childhood. Notification, intervention, and mitigation of those risks during our daily lives would, therefore, yield similar results in reducing chronic conditions.

B. *Virtual delivery of services*: A large portion of Health Guardian services may take place through enhanced use of technology and mobile devices. From information gathering, to virtual visits with the Health Guardians, PCPs or specialists, use of virtual methods would allow convenience, ease of access, and reduction of cost for access to essential care services. Technological advances such as biometric tracking through wearable devices can add to the richness of this virtual interface between the Health Guardians and the consumer.

C. *Elimination of waste and avoidance of unnecessary care*: Because of the financial alignment between Health Guardians and the consumer, Health Guardians would not profit from overuse of medical services. Consequently, this unified guardian-patient unit may navigate the maze of the sick care system using tools and information to reduce or avoid unnecessary care and waste. For example, when the consumer requires a lab or imaging, the Health Guardian can identify the nearest provider that offers the best price for the best quality. The Health Guardian may also arrange and participate in virtual visits with a specialist to ensure that the consumer is not overwhelmed by the complexity of medical issues. To draw an analogy, Health Guardians would act as a sherpa guide for the consumer to traverse the mountainous complexity of our hospital-based sick care system.

## Savings

A consumer who is in control of her healthcare decisions will be more engaged to remain healthy and reduce her chances of chronic conditions. By delivering essential care through Health Guardianship, and channeling the above-mentioned business principles, we would create savings that are estimated at 30%–50% of the existing healthcare expenses in the U.S. This would translate to savings of $3,000–$5,000 per capita, or between $1.5–$2 trillion in annual savings in healthcare spending in 2020. Such massive savings could be used to fund further research of health risks associated with chronic conditions, which would further improve the abilities of Health Guardians to develop better tools to mitigate health risks. Thus, the Health Guardian segment would create perpetual improvement and savings for payers of healthcare costs.

We have applied and implemented the above principles at BowTie Medical, the company I founded to find solutions for the problems of our healthcare system. For a better understanding of how the health guardianship works, please visit www.bowtiemedical.com.

CHAPTER 6

# HEALTH GUARDIANS WOULD INTEGRATE HEALTH RISK MANAGEMENT
## AND 21ST-CENTURY ADVANCEMENTS TO GUARD OUR HEALTH

To flesh out the key features of Health Guardianship, we must tap into the advancements brought about during the 20th century. By combining the democratization of health information with virtual delivery of health services that make communication with healthcare professionals readily accessible, we can create a series of goals and objectives for the structure and delivery of Health Guardianship.

The first objective would be to integrate clinical care, provided by a PCP, and other more common needs of an individual such as nutrition, fitness, and mental health into a BowTie risk management strategy. This structure for risk strategy would focus on health hazards such as obesity, diabetes, cardiovascular disease, musculoskeletal issues, and other chronic conditions and create tools and services that identify, reduce, or even eliminate the health and cost hazards associated with such chronic ailments. Individuals are exposed to these hazards as a result of their age, sex, socioeconomic status, behavior, habits, and mental health. Health Guardians would directly address these issues to keep the individual in their best health while also reducing healthcare costs.

Another element necessary to achieving the aims of Health Guardianship is the prioritization of a customized experience for each person who seeks Health Guardian services. Guarding one's health is meant to be a collaborative effort between an individual, her PCP, and a Health Guardian agent. Health Guardianship would provide the tools required to allow the individual to harness her autonomy to remain healthy. As people communicate with their banks or a financial advisor in order to keep financial stability, people would communicate with their Health Guardian to maintain their physical, emotional, and mental wellbeing on a daily basis. Whether an individual needs to keep track of the type and amount of food she is eating per day in order to maintain a healthy body weight, requires guidance on what physical exercise to perform to decrease osteoarthritis symptoms, or requires access to mental health counseling to work through stress, the Health Guardians would provide resources and access to care to address the issue.

Health Guardianship would also include virtual-based care and risk management strategies. In today's age, many goods we require throughout our day can be delivered with the press of a button online. From financial transactions, transportation and traveling, even to receiving groceries, society has developed systems to make "running errands" take a matter of minutes. The individual does not even have to leave her house. Through Health Guardianship, the same mode of delivery will be used to help an individual receive her health needs. For example, the virtual element of Health Guardianship might send an individual a daily meal plan to be accompanied with daily exercises. The Health Guardian, who would be tasked with mitigating or alleviating any existing chronic conditions, would also have access to this daily information and help the individual remain accountable. The hope is that the Health Guardian helps the individual reduce chronic conditions or stops them from developing them in the first place. In this way, the health hazard is minimized and managed as a part of the individual's daily routine, as naturally as tying our shoes before going outside.

To properly address an individual's unique health hazards and chronic conditions, Health Guardianship would also include personalized biometric and genetic information to extend the ability of risk management and improve results. Most if not all of the biological signals from our daily living (blood pressure, temperature, heart rate, heart rhythms, and various biometric elements in our serum such as sugar levels, our kidney, and liver function) can be obtained and digitally transferred to a health cloud that Health Guardian may access. When healthcare is customized to meet the needs of an individual based on her genetic, biometric, clinical, and environmental profiles, we will see positive and sustainable results.

Now, let's talk about how Health Guardians would be compensated. On this topic, the most important goal we must keep in mind is to ensure that there are no misalignments between the Health Guardian's financial motivations or incentives and the health of the individuals served, especially as such outcomes relate to frequency of utilization. The Health Guardian must be paid and rewarded in proportion to the quality of their customer service, the positive health outcomes of their assigned individuals, and the partnership they are able to generate with that individual.

How can people begin to sign up for Health Guardianship? The easiest path under the current regulations (without need for any changes that must go through Congress) is to fund it through the existing payer system of healthcare. To begin the Health Guardianship program, it may be offered as a part of an employer's health coverage sponsorship. Federally initiated programs such as ICHRAs, employee assistance programs (EAPs), or Health Savings Accounts (HSAs) could be used to fund Health Guardianship through programs compliant with the Employee Retirement Income Security Act (ERISA) of 1974.[123]

The structure and mission of Health Guardianship may also be integrated into the function of PCPs or private practices that are independent from the hospitals and its financial interests. For example, such practices exist in each community and can convert themselves to a direct payment method, a model that has been named as DPC.[124] DPCs may add additional services to their offerings such as mental health, nutritional consulting, exercise, and other methods of physical activities. Further, associations of DPCs could contract with other organizations who have developed innovative models and tools for health risk identification and modification. DPCs will need to become technologically advanced and offer virtual services to overcome the existing limitations associated with in-person offerings of this segment.

A recent increase in the prevalence of crowdsourcing and organizations that function as support groups suggests that this type of connectivity is a useful way to unite patients and problem solve together. PatientsLikeMe[125] is a great example of how crowdsourcing operates. At this website, individuals with similar experiences can share advice and information that they have learned to discover and adapt to the changes that could reduce or eliminate the burden of their conditions.

Crowdsourcing is obtaining information, help, and resources from a relatively large group of people. Nowadays, it is most prevalent in internet platforms where groups can instant message and share resources. These groups may consist of paid or unpaid individuals. There are a number of advantages to this concept: crowdsourcing is incredibly cost effective, there is no need for intense oversight from managers, and fresh perspectives are almost constantly available. Crowdsourcing has already been implemented to improve finances and gather information, and can now be expanded to support Health Guardianship.

Health Guardianship would take full advantage of 21st-century technological advancements to digitally integrate all of the components that serve an individual's health needs. The virtual delivery of health and associated services could be supported by a low monthly subscription fee. Similar to the monthly fee that most of us currently pay for cell phone services, television streaming services, or even monthly grocery subscriptions, Health Guardianship would be a subscription that provides access to health services until a specialist or surgical procedure is needed. This is equal to 90% of all medical needs in our lives, as Health Guardianship is inclusive of primary care services. With Health Guardians serving their purpose of keeping people healthy, the hospital system would continue to serve their intended functions of providing services to individuals who are already sick. With both systems operating under their intended purposes, hospitals can compete for business of sick care without the scorn of their intentions and misalignments between the quality of their outcomes and the price for each service.

If we can digitalize, demonetize, and democratize nearly all of the information relating to the maintenance and protection of our health, we will disrupt the current organization of healthcare and reduce the cost for consumers, employers, and even the government. We estimate about $2 trillion dollars would be saved per year with the implementation of Health Guardianship. These savings could be used for advancing research into the science of age reversal, identifying and mitigating risk factors for other causes of death in the country like cancer, and many other advancements that our current sick care model prevents us from achieving.

The National Institutes of Health (NIH) has an annual budget of about $35 billion per year.[126] This is less than 1% of the total amount our country spends on healthcare (in 2020 we spent $4 trillion on healthcare). Other industries have understood the changing of tides and the shift to more modern technology as a way of lowering costs and improving services. It is time that healthcare does the same. Organizations like Google, Apple, and Amazon spend at least 10% of revenue on research and development (R&D). Spending about 10% of revenue from healthcare would increase the budget of the NIH and other similar institutions by 10-fold or 1,000%. Can you imagine, with our brilliant scientists, what increasing R&D resources by 10-fold would do to our current system? As an academic, I can tell you that something close to magic could occur in the fight against diseases so far deemed incurable: Alzheimer's, cancer, and diabetes. Significant, tangible strides would be taken to allow us to live a full, happy, and healthy life beyond 100 years of age.

Lastly, implementing the proposed structure for Health Guardianship would require minimal changes in current regulations, and it could be easily managed through existing payer channels for employer or government sponsored programs.

CHAPTER 7

# BOWTIE HEALTH GUARDIANSHIP MOONSHOT:
## "LIVING A FULL LIFE, BEYOND 100," A TRANSFORMATIVE PURPOSE FOR OUR 21ST-CENTURY HEALTHCARE

Salim Ismail and Peter Diamandis have presented the concept of the "massive transformative purpose" (MTP) in innovation. This concept refers to a goal that leads to the exponential growth of organizations who aim to radically disrupt and change the direction of an industry and lower the cost of essential services during this new era of digitalization, easy access to information, and demonetization.[136]

These innovative thinkers propose that companies such as Google, Facebook, Amazon, Apple, and Tesla have achieved their extraordinary growth and impact in our lives by focusing on such transformative purposes, such as Google's objective to "organize the world's information,"[128] or Apple's goal to "bring the best computing products and supports to students, educators, designers, scientists, engineers, business persons and consumers in over 140 countries around the world."[129] Facebook aims "to give people the power to build community and bring the world closer together,"[130] while Tesla's priority is accelerating "the world's transition to sustainable energy."[131]

I would like to end this chapter by proposing that—based on my understanding as a surgeon-scientist familiar with human biology, as well as the advances in knowledge of pathophysiology of disease that we have made over the past 100 years and about the risks for chronic conditions, interactions between genetics, environmental factors (nature vs. nurture), and the amazing tools we have created to study and intervene at organ, tissue, cellular, and molecular levels—we can target a massive transformative purpose for the Health Guardianship: keeping people healthy for their entire lives. By shifting our strategy from a sick care-based healthcare system that benefits from diagnosis and treatment of diseases and chronic conditions **after** they have been established, to identifying and eliminating the risks for those chronic conditions and diseases through use of our expanded knowledge and technological advancements, we can live a healthy life, free from chronic conditions, beyond 100.

Seeing a picture of the annual stakeholder meetings of Berkshire Hathaway company on May 31, 2021 (below) that was chaired by the then 90-year-old Warren Buffett and vice chaired by 97-year-old Charlie Munger[127] reminded me of a real possibility for the MTP of Health Guardianship. During the 10th decade of their lives, these two gentlemen hosted one of the wealthiest organization's annual meetings, discussing and teaching the next four generations about how to be smart and make money!

There are plenty of examples of individuals who have lived beyond 100 and who are in good health. This evidence indicates that our bodies are biologically able to live beyond the age of 100 free from crippling chronic conditions.

Therefore, I propose that the transformative purpose of the Health Guardianship segment of our healthcare be: **"To empower everyone to live a full life, beyond 100!"**

I hope we have presented enough evidence in this book to convince you that not only are we capable of achieving this transformative purpose, but we must do so in order to save our healthcare system from ruining our nation's economy and all of its components that have contributed to a remarkable prosperity over the past 100 years. We must innovate and create a new segment of healthcare by creating a "Health Guardianship" segment to meet America's needs where public health departments and the hospital-based sick care system cannot. With this innovation, we would have the best chance at having the healthiest population, reducing the cost of our sick care system, and perhaps creating the next chapter of value and wealth generation for our country and the rest of the world.

# EPILOGUE

The concept of Health Guardianship has been the latest element for me in connecting the components needed to solve problems in U.S. healthcare. For a while, like many other authors and people concerned with problems of healthcare, I was looking for the culprit: the villain of healthcare. I have lived in Northeast Ohio for the past 20 years, where there are four hospital-based systems competing in the business of sick care for a population of approximately four million. Many physicians, surgeons, and other providers have switched from one system to another, bargaining for better pay or quality of work. As many of these providers (including myself) can attest, there is really no difference in the quality of inpatient or outpatient care, competency of the physicians or surgeons, or challenges of misalignment and all the obstacles facing the health of our population between these four systems. During the past 20 years, each of these hospital-based sick care systems have grown in physical and financial size anywhere from 200%–400%, and collectively collect $20 billion each year in revenue. I know for a fact that the health needs of the population in Northeast Ohio have not increased by that level, nor has this population become 200%–400% healthier because of growth of services of these hospitals. As a matter of fact, having these four sick care systems in Northeast Ohio did not slow the rate of COVID-19, nor did Northeast Ohio have a lower mortality rate or a better experience with testing during the months of the pandemic. These systems are deep in the business of sick care and continue to grow their sick care services. Regardless of what the CMS does in cost cutting, or what insurance companies have done in their price negotiations with hospital systems, the people of Northeast Ohio have paid the cost of 200%–400% growth of those systems from their earnings, as people of many other cities like Pittsburgh, New York, Boston, and Los Angeles have paid for similar systems in their cities.

Similarly, COVID-19, as the biggest health crisis of the past century, boosted the market trends that have helped move us beyond the current models of care delivery. The explosion of virtual delivery of acute care as part of primary care through several pioneering companies (TeleDoc, MD live, and AMwell) and market valuation of them (market capitalization of $5–$15 billion) is evidence that changing the healthcare system toward better and more affordable access has begun. Expansion of these services with other components of a more comprehensive primary care, such as management of chronic conditions and managing a person's health risks and issues, suggests that the system's innovation will continue. Other developments—like the expansion of DPC practices, medical cost sharing (Sedera and ministry-based organizations), market-driven forces such as the shift of employers as intermediaries in healthcare purchasers to sponsors of it (transformation from defined benefits to defined contribution), price transparency mandates, and many other innovations—have convinced me that we are entering a new era in evolution of our healthcare system. This new era is similar to the span of time from 1975 to 1985, which saw the initial but rapidly evolving steps of developing personal computers, digitalization and access to information, and computational power. This time also represents the era of 1990 to 2000 when the power of the internet was expanded. These two eras saw huge growth of companies such as Apple, Microsoft, Google, and Amazon. I believe we are entering into an era where companies that focus on system innovation for better and more affordable healthcare access, fair pricing, restoring the control of decisions to the individual, and removal of misalignments will change healthcare, like how the tech companies changed our professional and personal lives. The establishment of "Health Guardianship" is the beginning of this era that will create a more affordable, accessible, and equitable healthcare system for everyone and allow us to achieve our true biological potential of living a full life, free from chronic conditions, beyond 100 years old.

I'm very proud that our efforts in founding BowTie Medical represent an initial real-life version of a "Health Guardianship" organization. BowTie Medical has successfully assembled the components of clinical medicine, behavioral coaching, and mental health, and established a Health Guardianship function with innovative payment methods aligned with the members' needs to guard their health, and their pocketbook! BowTie

Medical's goal is to "prevent its members from becoming patients." This acknowledgement is not an advertisement for the company I have founded, but an illustration for readers of this book to see a real-life example of Health Guardianship. I am confident that by relying on the ingenuity of the American public and cleverness of our market, this movement will continue, and it will bring us a new model of healthcare where we can fulfill our goal of keeping people healthy and the transformative purpose of living a long, full life.

# APPENDICES

The following timetable provides a more detailed history of development of various segments of healthcare, for those who are interested.

## History of Medicine[83]

**2600 BC** The Egyptian Imhotep describes the diagnosis and treatment of 200 diseases

**500 BC** Alcmaeon of Croton distinguishes veins from arteries

**460 BC** Birth of Hippocrates, the Greek father of medicine, begins the scientific study of medicine and prescribes a form of aspirin

**300 BC** Diocles writes the first known anatomy book

**280 BC** Herophilus studies the nervous system

**130 AD** Birth of Galen: Greek physician to gladiators and Roman emperors

**60AD** Pedanius Dioscorides writes De Materia Medica

**910** Persian physician Rhazes identifies smallpox

**1010** Avicenna writes *The Book of Healing* and *The Canon of Medicine*

**1249** Roger Bacon invents spectacles

**1489** Leonardo da Vinci dissects corpses

**1543** Vesalius publishes findings on human anatomy in *De Humani Corporis Fabrica*

**1590** Zacharius Janssen invents the microscope

**1628** William Harvey publishes *Anatomical Studies of the Motion of the Heart and of the Blood in Animals*, which forms the basis for future research on blood vessels, arteries, and the heart

**1656** Sir Christopher Wren experiments with canine blood transfusions

**1670** Anton van Leeuwenhoek discovers blood cells

**1683** Anton van Leeuwenhoek observes bacteria

**1701** Giacomo Pylarini gives the first smallpox inoculations

**1747** James Lind publishes his *A Treatise of the Scurvy*, stating that citrus fruits prevent scurvy

**1763** Claudius Amyand performs the first successful appendectomy

**1796** Edward Jenner develops the process of vaccination for smallpox, the first vaccine for any disease

**1800** Sir Humphry Davy discovers the anesthetic properties of nitrous oxide

**1816** René Laennec invents the stethoscope

**1818** James Blundell performs the first successful transfusion of human blood

**1842** Crawford W. Long uses ether as a general anesthetic

**1844** Horace Wells uses nitrous oxide as an anesthetic

**1846** William Morton, a dentist, is the first to publish the process of using anesthetic properties of nitrous oxide

**1849** Elizabeth Blackwell is the first woman to gain a medical degree from Geneva College Medical Institution in New York

**1847** Ignaz Semmelweis discovers how to prevent the transmission of puerperal fever

**1853** Charles Gabriel Pravaz and Alexander Wood develop the syringe

**1857** Louis Pasteur identifies germs as cause of disease

**1867** Joseph Lister develops the use of antiseptic surgical methods and publishes *On the Antiseptic Principle of the Practice of Surgery*

**1870** Robert Koch and Louis Pasteur establish the germ theory of disease

**1879** First vaccine developed for cholera

**1881** First vaccine developed for anthrax by Louis Pasteur

**1882** First vaccine developed for rabies by Louis Pasteur

- Koch discovers the tubercle bacillus

**1887** First contact lenses developed

**1890** Emil von Behring discovers antitoxins and develops tetanus and diphtheria vaccines

**1895** Wilhelm Conrad Roentgen discovers X-rays

**1896** First vaccine developed for typhoid fever

**1897** First vaccine developed for bubonic plague

**1899** Felix Hoffman develops aspirin

**1901** Karl Landsteiner introduces the system to classify blood into A, B, AB, and O groups

**1913** Dr. Paul Dudley White pioneers the use of the electrocardiograph - ECG

**1921** Edward Mellanby discovers that lack of vitamin D in the diet causes rickets

- Earle Dickson invents the adhesive bandage

**1922** Insulin first used to treat diabetes

**1923** First vaccine developed for diphtheria

**1926** First vaccine developed for whooping cough

**1927** First vaccine developed for tuberculosis

- First vaccine developed for tetanus

**1928** Sir Alexander Fleming discovers penicillin

**1935** First vaccine developed for yellow fever

- Percy Lavon Julian synthesizes the medicines physostigmine for glaucoma and cortisone for rheumatoid arthritis

**1937** First vaccine developed for typhus

- Bernard Fantus pioneers the use of the first blood bank in Chicago

**1942** Dr. Karl Theodore Dussik publishes the first paper on medical ultrasonic - ultrasound

**1943** Selman A. Waksman discovers the antibiotic streptomycin

**1945** First vaccine developed for influenza

**1950** John Hopps invents the first cardiac pacemaker/ defibrillator in animals

**1952** Paul Zoll develops the first external cardiac pacemaker to stimulate the heart across a closed chest

- Jonas Salk develops the first polio vaccine
- Rosalind Franklin uses X-ray diffraction to study the structure of DNA

**1953** James Watson and Francis Crick work on the structure of the DNA molecule

**1954** Gertrude Elion patents a leukemia-fighting drug

- Dr. Joseph E. Murray performs the first kidney transplant

**1955** Jonas Salk develops the first polio vaccine

**1963** Thomas Fogarty invents the balloon embolectomy catheter

**1964** First vaccine developed for measles

**1967** First vaccine developed for mumps

- Dr. Christiaan Barnard performs the first human heart transplant

**1970** First vaccine developed for rubella

**1974** First vaccine developed for chicken pox

**1975** Robert S. Ledley invents whole-body CAT scan

**1977** First vaccine developed for pneumonia

**1978** First test-tube baby is born

- First vaccine developed for meningitis

**1980** Smallpox is eradicated

**1981** First vaccine developed for hepatitis B

**1983** HIV, the virus that causes AIDS, is identified

**1984** Alec Jeffreys devises a genetic fingerprinting method

**1985** Willem J. Kolff invents the artificial kidney dialysis machine

**1992** First vaccine developed for hepatitis A

**1996** Dolly the sheep becomes the first clone

**2006** First vaccine to target a cause of cancer

# APPENDIX

**Digitized:** Anything that becomes digitized enters the same exponential growth we see in computing. Digital information is easy to access, share, and distribute—it can spread at the speed of the internet. Once a product or service can be represented as "1's and 0's"—from biotechnology to music—it becomes an information-based technology and enters exponential growth.

**Deceptive:** Once something is digitized, its initial period of growth is deceptive because exponential trends don't seem to grow fast at first. Doubling .01 only gets you 0.2, then 0.4, and so on. At this phase, everything looks like "zero." But exponential growth really takes off after it breaks the whole-number barrier. 2 quickly becomes 32, which then becomes 32,000 before you know it.

**Disruptive**: The existing market for a given product or service is disrupted by the new market that the exponential technology creates because digital technologies outperform in terms of cost and effectiveness. Once you can stream music on your phone, why buy CDs or records? If you can also snap, store, and share photographs, why buy a camera and film?

**Demonetized**: Money is increasingly removed from the equation as the technology becomes cheaper—often to the point of being free. Software is less expensive to produce than hardware, and copies are virtually free. You can now download any number of apps on your phone to access terabytes of information and enjoy a multitude of services at costs approaching zero.

**Dematerialized**: Separate physical products are removed from the equation. Technologies that were once bulky or expensive—cameras, GPS, phones, maps—are now all in a smartphone that fits in your pocket.

**Democratized**: Once something is digitized, more people have access to it. Powerful technologies are no longer only for governments, large organizations, or the wealthy.

# BIBLIOGRAPHY

1. Barton, M. Imhotep - The First Physician. Past Medical History. May 28, 2016. Accessed June 2021. https://www.pastmedicalhistory.co.uk/imhotep-the-first-physician/

2. Bay, N. S., Bay, B. H. Greek anatomist herophilus: the father of anatomy. December 31, 2010. https://doi.org/10.5115/acb.2010.43.4.280

3. Connelly, D. A history of aspirin. September 26, 2014. Accessed June 2021. https://pharmaceutical-journal.com/article/infographics/a-history-of-aspirin

4. The Wood Library-Museum of Anesthesiology. History of Anesthesia. Accessed June 2021. https://www.woodlibrary-museum.org/history-of-anesthesia/

5.PBS. Opium Throughout History. Accessed June 2021. https://www.pbs.org/wgbh/pages/frontline/shows/heroin/etc/history.html

6. Brazier, Y. Ancient Egyptian medicine. November 16, 2018. Accessed June 2021. https://www.medicalnewstoday.com/articles/323633

7. Wall, B.M. History of Hospitals. Accessed May 2021. https://www.nursing.upenn.edu/nhhc/nurses-institutions-caring/history-of-hospitals/

8. O'mara, K. Feb. 11, 1752: First hospital in the U.S. opens (it's still standing). February 11, 2014. https://yhoo.it/3z2Y5C5

9. Manoli-Skocay, Constance. A Gentle Death: Tuberculosis. Winter 2003. Accessed May 2021. https://concordlibrary.org/special-collections/essays-on-concord-history/a-gentle-death-tuberculosis-in-19th-century-concord

10. U.S. Department of Health and Human Services. Accessed June 2021. https://www.hhs.gov/

11. Assistant Secretary of Health. Accessed June 2021. https://en.wikipedia.org/wiki/United_States_Department_of_Health_and_Human_Services

12. United States Public Health Service Commissioned Corps. Accessed June 2021. https://en.wikipedia.org/wiki/United_States_Public_Health_Service_Commissioned_Corps

13. Uniformed services of the United States. Accessed June 2021. https://en.wikipedia.org/wiki/Uniformed_services_of_the_United_States

14. Marine Hospital Service. Accessed June 2021. https://en.wikipedia.org/wiki/Marine_Hospital_Service

15. Milliman Report 2022- https://www.milliman.com/-/media/milliman/pdfs/2022-articles/2022-milliman-medical-index.ashx

16. Public Health Service Act, 1944. Accessed June 2021. https://www.ncbi.nlm.nih.gov/pmc/articles/PMC1403520/

17. Gaziano TA, Suhrcke M, Brouwer E, et al. Costs and Cost-Effectiveness of Interventions and Policies to Prevent and Treat Cardiovascular and Respiratory Diseases. In: Prabhakaran D, Anand S, Gaziano TA, et al., editors. Cardiovascular, Respiratory, and Related Disorders. 3rd edition. Washington (DC): The International Bank for Reconstruction and Development / The World Bank; 2017 Nov 17. Chapter 19. Available from: https://www.ncbi.nlm.nih.gov/books/NBK525142/ doi: 10.1596/978-1-4648-0518-9_ch19)

18. Preventive healthcare. Accessed June 2021. https://en.wikipedia.org/wiki/Preventive_healthcare

19. Anderson JG, Abrahamson K. Your Health Care May Kill You: Medical Errors. Stud Health Technol Inform. 2017;234:13-17. PMID: 28186008

20. Medical error—the third leading cause of death in the US: BMJ 2016;353:i2139

21. Marine Corps Uniforms and Symbols. Accessed June 2021. https://www.marines.com/about-the-marine-corps/who-are-the-marines/uniforms-symbols.html

22. Military Rank. Accessed June 2021. https://en.wikipedia.org/wiki/Military_rank

23. Gale AH. Bigger but not better: hospital mergers increase costs and do not improve quality. Mo Med. 2015 Jan-Feb;112(1):4-5. PMID: 25812261; PMCID: PMC6170097.

24. Kaiser Family Foundation: The Facts on Medicare Spending and Financing https://www.kff.org/ad80ea6/

25. Baltimore City Health Department. About The Baltimore City Health Department. Accessed June 2021. https://health.baltimorecity.gov/node/20

26. Institute of Medicine (US) Committee for the Study of the Future of Public Health. The Future of Public Health. Accessed June 2021. https://www.ncbi.nlm.nih.gov/books/NBK218212/

27. KFF: Issue brief 9510-2; what we know about provider consolidation-https://www.kff.org/1677a2e/

28. National Association of County and City Health Officials. Operational Definition of a Functional Local Health Department. Accessed July 2021.

29. American Red Cross. History of Blood Transfusions. Accessed May 2021. https://www.redcrossblood.org/do-

nate-blood/blood-donation-process/what-happens-to-donated-blood/blood-transfusions/history-blood-transfusion.html

30. Columbia Surgery. History of Medicine: Dr. Roentgen's Accidental X-Rays. Accessed May 2021. https://columbiasurgery.org/news/2015/09/17/history-medicine-dr-roentgen-s-accidental-x-rays

31. Robinson, D., Toledo, A. Historical development of modern anesthesia. Accessed May 2021. https://pubmed.ncbi.nlm.nih.gov/22583009/

32. Committee on Public Health Strategies to Improve Health; Institute of Medicine. For the Public's Health: Investing in a Healthier Future. April 20 2012. Accessed May 2021. https://www.ncbi.nlm.nih.gov/books/NBK201025/

33. Schumann, J. A Bygone Era: When Bipartisanship Led to Health Care Transformation. October 2, 2016. Accessed May 2021. https://www.npr.org/sections/health-shots/2016/10/02/495775518/a-bygone-era-when-bipartisanship-led-to-health-care-transformation

34. Benner, P. A Brief History of Insurance. September 8, 2017. Accessed May 2021. https://northstarpolicy.org/brief-history-insurance

35. Mihm, S. Employer-based health care was a wartime accident. February 24, 2017. Accessed May 2021. https://www.chicagotribune.com/opinion/commentary/ct-obamacare-health-care-employers-20170224-story.html

36. Tax Policy Center. Major Enacted Tax Legislation, 1940-1949. Accessed May 2021. https://www.taxpolicycenter.org/laws-proposals/major-enacted-tax-legislation-1940-1949

37. Blakey, R., Blakey, G. The Federal Revenue Act of 1942. Accessed May 2021. https://www.jstor.org/stable/1949066

38. Blumenthal, D., Gustaffson, L., Bishop, S., To Control Health Care Costs, U.S. Employers Should Form Purchasing Alliances. November 2, 2018. Accessed May 2021. https://hbr.org/2018/11/to-control-health-care-costs-u-s-employers-should-form-purchasing-alliances

39. Harry S. Truman Library and Museum. The Challenge of National Healthcare. Accessed June 2021. https://www.trumanlibrary.gov/education/presidential-inquiries/challenge-national-healthcare

40. National Health Law Program. 1965 - The Medicare and Medicaid Act. July 30, 1965. Accessed June 2021. https://healthlaw.org/announcement/medicare-and-medicaid-act-1965-2/

41. Himber, V. How Many Americans Get Health Insurance from their Employer? January 11, 2021. Accessed June 2021. https://www.ehealthinsurance.com/resources/small-business/how-many-americans-get-health-insurance-from-their-employer

42. Medicare and Medicaid: Keeping Us Healthy for 50 Years. Accessed June 2021. https://www.cms.gov/Out-

reach-and-Education/Look-Up-Topics/50th-Anniversary/Long-Form-Drop-In-Article.pdf

43. Edwards, A., Sherer Greenbaum, L. Around the World in Healthcare Systems: Europe. Accessed June 2021. https://www.mmc.com/insights/publications/2021/february/around-the-world-in-healthcare-systems-europe.html

44. U.S. Department of Health and Human Services. Health Insurance. Accessed June 2021. https://www.hhs.gov/programs/health-insurance/index.html

45. U.S. Department of Veteran Affairs. March 15, 2021. Accessed June 2021. https://www.va.gov/health-care/

46. Rosso, R. U.S. Health Care Coverage and Spending. January 26, 2021. Accessed June 2021. https://sgp.fas.org/crs/misc/IF10830.pdf

47. Glied, S., Zhu, B. Catastrophic Out-of-Pocket Health Care Costs. April 17, 2020. Accessed June 2021. https://www.commonwealthfund.org/publications/issue-briefs/2020/apr/catastrophic-out-of-pocket-costs-problem-middle-income

48. Centers for Medicare & Medicaid Services. CMS Office of the Actuary Releases 2019 National Health Expenditures. December 16, 2020. Accessed June 2021. https://www.cms.gov/newsroom/press-releases/cms-office-actuary-releases-2019-national-health-expenditures

49. Rosenthal, Elisabeth. 2018. *An American Sickness: how healthcare became a big business and how you can take it back.*

50. Hospitals by Ownership Type. 2019. Accessed July 2021. https://www.kff.org/other/state-indicator/hospitals-by-ownership/?currentTimeframe=0&sortModel=%7B%22colId%22:%22Location%22,%22sort%22:%22asc%22%7D

51. Healthcare fast facts. Accessed July 2021. https://alight.com/research-insights/largest-hospital-systems-in-america

52. Open The Books. Top 82 U.S. Non-Profit Hospitals: Quantifying Government Payments and Financial Assets. June 24, 2019. Accessed July 2021. https://www.openthebooks.com/top-82-us-non-profit-hospitals-quantifying-government-payments-and-financial-assets--open-the-books-oversight-report/

53. Myers, Brady. "Trends in the medical stop-loss market." MVP Roundtable. 2019.

54. Health Care in the United States: Your Essential Guide. September 2, 2020. Accessed July 2021. https://meritagemed.com/healthcare-in-the-united-states/

55. Trend Tables. 2019. Accessed August 2021. https://www.cdc.gov/nchs/data/hus/2019/044-508.pdf

56. Kamal, R., Ramirez, G., Cox, C. How does health spending in the U.S. compare to other countries. December 23, 2020. Accessed July 2021. https://www.healthsystem-

tracker.org/chart-collection/health-spending-u-s-compare-countries/#item-start

57. The Commonwealth Fund. U.S. Health Care from a Global Perspective, 2019: Higher Spending, Worse Outcomes? January 30, 2020. Accessed July 2021. https://www.commonwealthfund.org/publications/issue-briefs/2020/jan/us-health-care-global-perspective-2019

58. Feldscher, K., What's behind high U.S. healthcare costs. March 13, 2018. Accessed July 2021. https://news.harvard.edu/gazette/story/2018/03/u-s-pays-more-for-health-care-with-worse-population-health-outcomes/

59. Centers for Disease Control and Prevention. About Chronic Diseases. April 28, 2021. Accessed May 2021. https://www.cdc.gov/chronicdisease/about/index.htm#:~:text=Related%20Pages,disability%20in%20the%20United%20States.

60. Centers for Disease Control and Prevention. Overweight and Obesity. Accessed June 2021. https://www.cdc.gov/obesity/index.html

61. Centers for Disease Control and Prevention. Diabetes and Prediabetes. Accessed June 2021. https://www.cdc.gov/chronicdisease/resources/publications/factsheets/diabetes-prediabetes.htm

62. Centers for Disease Control and Prevention. Arthritis National Statistics. February 7, 2018. Accessed June 2021.

https://www.cdc.gov/arthritis/data_statistics/national-statistics.html

63. Centers for Disease Control and Prevention. Alzheimer's Disease and Healthy Aging. October 26, 2020. Accessed June 2021. https://www.cdc.gov/aging/aginginfo/alzheimers.htm

64. Centers for Disease Control and Prevention. Depression. September 13, 2021. Accessed June 2021. https://www.cdc.gov/nchs/fastats/depression.htm

65. Waters, H., Graf, M., The Costs of Chronic Disease in the U.S. August 28. Accessed June 2021. https://milkeninstitute.org/report/costs-chronic-disease-us#:~:text=Key%20findings%3A,percent%20of%20the%20nation's%20GDP.

66. Campbell, O. Here's what happened when Ronald Reagan went after healthcare programs. It's not good. September 13, 2017. Accessed July 2021. https://timeline.com/reagan-trump-healthcare-cuts-8cf64aa242eb

67. Frakt, A. Reagan, Deregulation and America's Exceptional Rise in Health Care Costs. June 4, 2018. Accessed May 2021. https://www.nytimes.com/2018/06/04/upshot/reagan-deregulation-and-americas-exceptional-rise-in-health-care-costs.html

68. Diagnosis Related Group (DRG). July 13, 2018. Accessed May 2021. https://hmsa.com/portal/provider/zav_pel.fh.DIA.650.htm

69. Plaut, T., Arons, B., President Clinton's proposal for health care reform: key provisions and issues. Accessed May 2021. https://pubmed.ncbi.nlm.nih.gov/7989016/

70. Gottlieb, S. The Clintonian Roots of Obamacare. Summer 2015. Accessed May 2021. https://www.nationalaffairs.com/publications/detail/the-clintonian-roots-of-obamacare

71. The Bush Record. Empowering Medicare Beneficiaries With Affordable Options. Accessed May 2021. https://georgewbush-whitehouse.archives.gov/infocus/bushrecord/factsheets/medicare.html

72. Medicare Advantage Plans. Accessed May 2021. https://www.medicare.gov/sign-up-change-plans/types-of-medicare-health-plans/medicare-advantage-plans

73. U.S. Department of Health and Human Services. About the Affordable Care Act. March 23, 2021. Accessed May 2021. https://www.hhs.gov/healthcare/about-the-aca/index.html

74. O'Donnell, J. Red and Blue America see eye-to-eye on one issue: the nation's health care system needs fixing. February 7, 2020. Accessed July 2021. https://www.usatoday.com/story/news/health/2020/02/07/remove-buzzwords-health-care-debate-americans-find-common-ground/4601892002/

75. Hackbarth, A., Berwick, M., Eliminating Waste in U.S. Health Care. April 11, 2012. Accessed May 2021. https://jamanetwork.com/journals/jama/article-abstract/1148376

76. Federal Register. Improving Price and Quality Transparency in American Healthcare To Put Patients First. June 27, 2021. Accessed August 2021. https://www.federalregister.gov/documents/2019/06/27/2019-13945/improving-price-and-quality-transparency-in-american-healthcare-to-put-patients-first

77. Gale, Arthur. John Wennberg, MD: The Influential Doctor Who Blames Physicians and Fee-For-Service Medicine for the High Cost of Health Care. May - June 2016. Accessed August 2021. https://www.ncbi.nlm.nih.gov/pmc/articles/PMC6140041/

78. Daniel, M. Study Suggests Medical Errors Now Third Leading Cause of Death in the U.S. May 3, 2016. Accessed July 2021. https://www.hopkinsmedicine.org/news/media/releases/study_suggests_medical_errors_now_third_leading_cause_of_death_in_the_us

79. Kohn, L., Corrigan, J., Donaldson, M. To Err is Human: Building a Safer Health System. 2000. Accessed August 2021. https://pubmed.ncbi.nlm.nih.gov/25077248/

80. JAMA Network. Less is More. https://jamanetwork.com/collections/44045/less-is-more

81. Gawanda, A. Overkill: An avalanche of unnecessary medical care is harming patients physically and financially. What can we do about it? May 20, 2015. Accessed August 2021. https://psnet.ahrq.gov/issue/overkill-avalanche-unnec-

essary-medical-care-harming-patients-physically-and-financially-what

82. Collins, S., Radley, D., Baumgartner, J., Trends in Employer Health Care Coverage, 2008-2018: Higher Costs for Workers and Their Families. November 21, 2019. Accessed August 2021. https://www.commonwealthfund.org/publications/2019/nov/trends-employer-health-care-coverage-2008-2018

83. Anderson JG, Abrahamson K. Your Health Care May Kill You: Medical Errors. Stud Health Technol Inform. 2017;234:13-17. PMID: 28186008

84. Hospital Acquisition of Physician Practices Drive Up Cost. https://www.ahip.org/news/articles/hospital-acquisition-of-physician-practices-drives-up-cost

85. Marks, Jay. Medical Definition of Hippocratic Oath. June 3, 2021. Accessed July 2021. https://www.medicinenet.com/hippocratic_oath/definition.htm

86. Schwartz, E. Don't Let Your Doctor Kill You: How to Beat Physician Arrogance, Corporate Greed and a Broken System. 2015.

87. Our Mission. https://www.choosingwisely.org/our-mission/

88. A Timeline of COVID-19 Developments. January 1, 2021. Accessed May 2021. https://www.ajmc.com/view/a-timeline-of-covid19-developments-in-2020

89. Szmigiera, M. GDP Loss due to COVID-19, by economy 2020. June 1 2021. Accessed June 2021. https://www.statista.com/statistics/1240594/gdp-loss-covid-19-economy/

90. COVID Data Tracker Weekly Review. September 17, 2021. Accessed September 2021. https://www.cdc.gov/coronavirus/2019-ncov/covid-data/covidview/index.html

91. American Diabetes Association. Diabetes and Coronavirus. Accessed June 2021. https://www.diabetes.org/coronavirus-covid-19

92. Centers for Disease Control and Prevention. Obesity, Race/Ethnicity, and COVID-19. https://www.cdc.gov/obesity/data/obesity-and-covid-19.html

93. Centers for Disease Control and Prevention. Body Mass Index and Risk for COVID-19–Related Hospitalization, Intensive Care Unit Admission, Invasive Mechanical Ventilation, and Death — United States, March–December 2020. March 12, 2021. Accessed June 2021. https://www.cdc.gov/mmwr/volumes/70/wr/mm7010e4.htm

94. Weber, Lauren. Laura Ungar, The Associated Press, Hannah Recht, and Anna Maria Berry-Jester. Hollowed-Out Public Health System Faces More Cuts Amid Virus. July 1, 2020. Accessed June 2021. https://khn.org/news/us-public-health-system-underfunded-under-threat-faces-more-cuts-amid-covid-pandemic/

95. Institute of Medicine (US) Committee for the Study of the Future of Public Health. The Future of Public Health.

Washington (DC): National Academies Press (US); 1988. Available from: https://www.ncbi.nlm.nih.gov/books/NBK218218/ doi: 10.17226/1091

96. N Engl J Med, Vol. 344, No. 26. June 28, 2001. Accessed July 2021. www.nejm.org

97. Centers for Disease Control and Prevention. Heart Disease and Stroke. October 7, 2020. Accessed June 2021. https://www.cdc.gov/chronicdisease/resources/publications/factsheets/heart-disease-stroke.htm

98. Centers for Disease Control and Prevention. Health and Economic Costs of Chronic Diseases. June 23, 2021. Accessed July 2021. https://www.cdc.gov/chronicdisease/about/costs/index.htm

99. Centers for Disease Control and Prevention. Tobacco Use. June 16, 2021. September 18, 2021. https://www.cdc.gov/chronicdisease/resources/publications/factsheets/tobacco.htm

100. Centers for Disease Control and Prevention. Poor Nutrition. January 11, 2021. Accessed July 2021. https://www.cdc.gov/chronicdisease/resources/publications/factsheets/nutrition.htm

101. Centers for Disease Control and Prevention. Lack of Physical Activity. September 25, 2019. Accessed July 2021. https://www.cdc.gov/chronicdisease/resources/publications/factsheets/physical-activity.htm

102. Centers for Disease Control and Prevention. Excessive Alcohol Use. September 21, 2020. Accessed July 2021. https://www.cdc.gov/chronicdisease/resources/publications/factsheets/alcohol.htm

103. Locsin, A. Is Air Travel Safer Than Car Travel? Accessed July 2021. https://traveltips.usatoday.com/advantages-air-travel-12486.html

104. Reinberg, S. Angelina Jolie Has Preventative Double Mastectomy. May 14, 2013. Accessed July 2021. https://www.medicinenet.com/script/main/art.asp?articlekey=169836

105. Alzheimer's Disease- Epidemiology and Burden. April 28, 2016. Accessed June 2021. https://institute.progress.im/en/content/epidemiology-and-burden%E2%80%8B

106. Mobile Fact Sheet. April 7, 2021. https://www.pewresearch.org/internet/fact-sheet/mobile/

107. Pros and Cons of Health Websites. December 5, 2017. https://www.canopyhealth.com/en/members/articles/the-pros-and-cons-of-health-websites.html

108. Eskew PM, Klink K. Direct Primary Care: Practice Distribution and Cost Across the Nation. J Am Board Fam Med. 2015 Nov-Dec;28(6):793-801. doi: 10.3122/jabfm.2015.06.140337. PMID: 26546656.

109. Porter, Michael E. PhD Value-Based Health Care Delivery, Annals of Surgery: October 2008 - Volume 248 - Issue 4 - p 503-509 doi: 10.1097/SLA.0b013e31818a43af

110. Gawande, A. Why Doctors Hate Their Computers. November 5, 2018. Accessed June 2021. https://www.newyorker.com/magazine/2018/11/12/why-doctors-hate-their-computers

111. Brothers, W. A Timeline of COVID-19 Vaccine Development. December 3, 2020. Accessed June 2021. https://www.biospace.com/article/a-timeline-of-covid-19-vaccine-development/

112. Faulkner, B. How Google Is Impacting Healthcare In The Digital Age. Accessed July 2021. https://getreferralmd.com/2019/08/how-google-is-impacting-healthcare-in-the-digital-age/

113. Guarino, A. Study finds 89% of US citizens turn to Google before their doctor. June 24, 2019. Accessed June 2021. https://www.wect.com/2019/06/24/study-finds-us-citizens-turn-google-before-their-doctor/

114. Survey Reveals How COVID-19 Pandemic Has Impacted Millennial Health. https://www.harmonyhit.com/survey-reveals-how-covid-19-pandemic-has-impacted-millennial-health/

115. Trends in the Use of Telehealth During the Emergence of the COVID-19 Pandemic — United States, Janu-

ary–March 2020. October 30, 2020. Accessed June 2021. https://www.cdc.gov/mmwr/volumes/69/wr/mm6943a3.htm

116. The Discovery of the Double Helix. https://profiles.nlm.nih.gov/spotlight/sc/feature/doublehelix

117. Ryan, J. CRISPR gene-editing treatment shows success in first human patients. November 19, 2019. https://www.cnet.com/news/crispr-gene-editing-treatment-shows-success-in-first-human-patients/

118. Kelly, S. Robotic surgeries surge to 15% of all procedures, despite limited evidence. January 14, 2020. https://www.medtechdive.com/news/robotic-surgeries-surge-to-15-of-all-procedures-despite-limited-evidence/570370/

119. The 10 Hottest Medical Technologies in 2021. Accessed August 2021. https://www.medicaltechnologyschools.com/medical-lab-technician/top-new-health-technologies

120. We Are Xprise. https://www.xprize.org/

121. Singularity University. https://www.su.org/

122. 1903 - The First Flight. April 14, 2015. Accessed July 2021. https://www.nps.gov/wrbr/learn/historyculture/the-firstflight.htm

123. U.S. Department of Labor. Employee Retirement Income Security Act (ERISA). https://www.dol.gov/general/topic/retirement/erisa

124. Direct Primary Care Coalition. https://www.dpcare.org/

125. PatientsLikeMe. https://www.patientslikeme.com/

126. National Institute of Health. Budget. https://www.nih.gov/about-nih/what-we-do/budget

127. Li, Yun., Pound, J., Fitzgerald, M. Here's a full recap of the best moments from Warren Buffet at Berkshire Hathaway's annual meeting. May 3, 2021. Accessed July 2021. https://www.cnbc.com/2021/05/01/berkshire-hathaway-meeting-live-updates.html

128. About Google. https://about.google/

129. Rowland, C. Apple Inc.'s Mission Statement and Vision Statement (An Analysis). September 23, 2020. Accessed August 2021. http://panmore.com/apple-mission-statement-vision-statement

130. Facebook. FAQs. https://investor.fb.com/resources/default.aspx#:~:text=Facebook%20Investor%20Relations%3F-,What%20is%20Facebook's%20mission%20statement%3F,express%20what%20matters%20to%20them.

131. About Tesla. https://www.tesla.com/about

132. "Medicare Advantage, Direct Contracting, And The Medicare 'Money Machine,' Part 1: The Risk-Score Game," Health Affairs Blog, September 29, 2021.

133. Rosenthal, E. Paying Till It Hurts. 2014-2015. Accessed August 2021. https://www.nytimes.com/interactive/2014/health/paying-till-it-hurts.html

134. Papanicolas, I., Marino, A., Lorenzoni, L., Jha, A. Comparison of Health Care Spending by Age in 8 High Income Countries. August 3, 2020. Accessed July 2021. https://www.ncbi.nlm.nih.gov/pmc/articles/PMC7411536/

135. New England Journal of Medicine. Ecology of Healthcare. June 28, 2001. Accessed August 2021. www.nejm.org

136. Ismail, S. Exponential Organizations. October 4, 2014. Accessed August 2021. https://www.google.com/books/edition/Exponential_Organizations/OprNBAAAQBAJ?hl=en&gbpv=1&printsec=frontcover

137. Catastrophic Care- Why Everything We Think We Know About Health Care is Wrong- By David Goldhill- 2013 Knopf Doubleday Publishing Group-(ISBN 9780345802736, 034580273X)

138. Centers for Medicare and Medicaid: What are the valued based programs? https://www.cms.gov/Medicare/Quality-Initiatives-Patient-Assessment-Instruments/Value-Based-Programs/Value-Based-Programs

139. Milton Freedman- How to cure health care- Hoover Institute-July 30, 2001- https://www.hoover.org/research/how-cure-health-care-0

# ACKNOWLEDGEMENTS

The learning that created this book is thoroughly the result of a lifelong personal and professional journey in life, which has been shaped by many individuals:

Immigration of our family to the U.S. was the first and riskiest step. My parents, Mostafa and Molouktadj Daneshgari, left the comfort of their homeland, Iran, to allow their children—I am the third of four children—to live and work in the U.S., where freedom, rule of law, and separation of church and government has created an eternal conduit for prosperity. Without my parents' sacrifices, and the support of my siblings (Khosrow, Parviz and Venus), I would not be writing these notes today.

My brother Parviz Daneshgari, an innovative thinker and a student of the late Dr. W. Edwards Deming, who has been my mentor in exploring how dysfunctions in a system would lead to waste and all its long-term complications.

The thousands of patients who trusted me with their medical and surgical care, and the hundreds of students (medical/college), residents, fellows, colleagues, and friends who helped me understand the complexities of the healthcare system, guided me to become a leader in the sick care system, and later encouraged me to become an entrepreneur to build a healthcare solution. I especially acknowledge E. David Crawford, Marty Koyle, the late Andrew Novick, the late Achilles Demetrious, Alan Wein, Adonis Hijaz, Tara Frenkle, Courtney Moore, Luis Moy, Guiming Liu, Nan Xiao, Yihao Lin, Sam Thomas, Christian Able, Paul Sems, Tony Dale, and Ben Matin.

Bernard Evenhuis, who is completing his medical school training and has been an inspiration to me as he embodies talents, energy, and the changes we will see in the next generation of physicians—those who will be guardians of health and not merely a cog in the wheel of a sick care system. Bernard will take the message of this book to its next stage.

I could have not made the radical changes in my personal and professional life without the unconditional support of my wife, Kristin Daneshgari, and the continuous energy I get from my children, Zal and Riya Daneshgari, who carry my hopes and dreams for the future.

My entire life's vision and mission has been shaped by Massoud and Maryam Rajavi's vision, actions, and guidance; the leaders who have taught me the art and science of conscious changes in life, and what must be done can be done.

# ABOUT THE AUTHOR

Firouz Daneshgari, MD, is a surgeon-scientist and an executive-entrepreneur who has continuously built upon his deep understanding and passion for innovations in healthcare toward more efficient, value-driven and scientifically mapped services and products. Trained at University of Tehran, Loyola Medical Center, University of Chicago, University of Colorado, Texas Southwestern Medical Center, and Case Western Reserve University (CWRU), Dr. Daneshgari rapidly rose in ranks as a successful surgeon-scientist, and visionary leader working at University of Colorado, Cleveland Clinic, and Case Western Reserve University. During the academic phase of his career, he operated on thousands of patients, published more than 200 scientific articles, led numerous scientific and clinical expert panels at the national and international levels, and trained over 100 students, residents, fellows, and junior faculty.

Dr. Daneshgari founded the first fellowship program in Female Pelvic Medicine & Reconstructive Surgery at Cleveland Clinic in 2001 and promoted it as a new joint subspeciality between urology and gynecology until it received accreditation from ACGME as a new Board Certification in 2011. As the third Chairman of Urology at CWRU, he founded the Urology Institute at University Hospitals of Cleveland, which rapidly rose through the *U.S. News & World Report* standings from being a program with no ranking to the honor roll (top 20) among 5,000 programs, and became among the top 10 clinical departments receiving NIH funding within three years of his leadership.

Following implementation of the Affordable Care Act and approval of its mandates by the Supreme Court during 2010-2012, Dr. Daneshgari founded BowTie Medical, an innovative company to create systematic innovations for bringing efficiency and value into the healthcare delivery system by reducing waste and improving the health of individuals. Under his leadership, relying on his innate knowledge of deficiencies of the current healthcare system, BowTie Medical has developed potential for exponential growth with delivery of innovative products and services such as **Virtual Comprehensive Care** and **Health Guardianship**.

In addition to this book, Dr. Daneshgari describes the components of his views on healthcare and the innovative path forward for creation of an efficient, value-driven and customer-controlled healthcare through a series of podcasts named "Why Can't We Have It All: The Missing Pieces in Our Healthcare" (www.wcwha.com).

CPSIA information can be obtained
at www.ICGtesting.com
Printed in the USA
JSHW032138080323
38670JS00003B/18